A PATCHWORK CHRISTMAS

By Margit Echols

A PATCHWORK CHRISTMAS

By Margit Echols

Sedgewood® Press
New York

Acknowledgments
I wish to thank those friends and colleagues who worked with me on the quilts: Emiko Loeb, who helped me piece the Christmas Pine and Whirling Pine; Karen Felicity Berkenfeld, who quilted the Christmas Pine; and Karen and Diane Rode Schneck, who helped me quilt the Feathered Star. As with quilters of the past, working together made the hours fly by while we settled matters of state and all manner of personal and social issues. And thanks to Jean Tofani for everything.

Credits: The author wishes to thank the following suppliers for generously providing many of the products used in the making of *A Patchwork Christmas*:
Batting and pillow forms: Mountain Mist "Fiber Loft," courtesy of the Stearns Technical Textile Co., 100 Williams St., Cincinnati, OH 45215-6316. ***Fabrics:*** Concord Home Sewing Fabrics, 1359 Broadway, New York, NY 10018; Laura Ashley Inc., 714 Madison Ave., New York, NY 10021; Peter Pan Fabrics, 1071 Avenue of the Americas, New York, NY 10018; V.I.P., division of Cranston Print Works Co., 1412 Broadway, New York, NY 10018.

For Sedgewood® Press:

Director: Elizabeth P. Rice
Project Editor: Ciba Vaughan
Associate Editor: Leslie Gilbert
Production Manager: Bill Rose
Design: Remo Cosentino
Photography: Schecter Lee

Distributed by Macmillan Publishing Company, a division of Macmillan, Inc.

ISBN: 0-02-496830-7
Library of Congress Catalog Card Number: 86-061601

Printed in the United States of America

10 9 8 7 6 5 4 3 2 1

Dedication

To Jane Norman, who crystallized my understanding of geometry. This book, particularly the last chapter, could not have been written without having known her and worked with her. She also introduced me to Verdalee.

And to Verdalee Tombelaine, my guardian angle [*sic*]. She was responsible for the exhibition of my work at the Horticultural Society of New York in 1981. It was for this show that the designs in *A Patchwork Christmas* were created.

Contents

Introduction

Several years ago I was honored with an invitation to exhibit my work in my first one-woman show. Because it was to be at the Horticultural Society of New York, the theme had to be floral or vegetal; because it was to take place during the Christmas season, I was faced with a double challenge.

As I had not already produced work of this kind, everything had to be designed from scratch. I began by adding a tree trunk to the base of a triangle — a simple tree shape that became the basis for many of the designs for the show. Other designs were taken directly from nature. The result: *A Patchwork Christmas*, which I now, with pleasure, share with you.

The first two chapters are instructional, covering in detail the basic techniques of quilting and pillow making. Succeeding chapters present more than 40 designs — from the simple to the complex, with step-by-step instructions, diagrams, and full-size patterns — that fit a wide range of holiday and gift-giving needs.

The first design is a quick and easy Christmas Tree Border for decorating a variety of ready-made items such as dinner napkins, towels and aprons.

The Christmas tree ornaments will help create a real old-fashioned country tree. You can cover your tree entirely with hearts in every imaginable combination of prints, plaids, stripes and trims, or you can dress your tree with angels in pretty calico gowns. A combination of stars, trees, houses, hearts and angels on a tree is also very special. Most of the designs are simple, others have more pieces, but none are hard to make.

Other projects that are simple yet decorative are the Christmas Stockings and Holiday Heart designs.

The stuffed calico fruits and vegetables in the Food Stuffs section are a perfect harvest centerpiece for any holiday table or sideboard. Hang the apples, pears and oranges from the tree, or tie them to a Christmas wreath. Put them on plates as party favors, or tie them with ribbons to gift packages. Give them as toys for children who will learn to love their veggies at an early age; they are soft, safe and fun to play with. Use them as fund raisers at craft fairs and bazaars. In bowls or baskets they will be at home anywhere, any time of year.

Part of the charm of the calico designs is the cheerful, humorous effect they have. Even the real thing, more beautiful than anything we could create, doesn't have the witty touch of calico.

The last section — a collection of traditional patchwork designs presented in new and imaginative ways — begins with the simplest design and ends with the most challenging, a progression in which one design becomes preparation for the next. It's possible to start anywhere, but by starting at the beginning, even a novice can understand how most complex designs are built on simple structures.

The Feathered Star, traditionally a showcase for the advanced quiltmaker, provides unlimited possibilities for experimenting with pattern and color. The basic star is broken down into parts that can be arranged in any number of combinations. Add to that all the choices color has to offer, and no two stars need ever be the same.

Whatever your preference, there's plenty to choose from that will offer many hours of pleasure and the opportunity to show off your best work.

SOURCE LIST

Quilting stencils for the Feathered Star quilt courtesy Stencils and Stuff, 72-12th St., NW, Strasburg, OH 44680.

Stencils for the Christmas Pine quilt and other supplies courtesy Come Quilt With Me, Inc., Box 1063, Brooklyn, NY 11202.

Quilting hoop courtesy Norwood Looms, Inc., Box 167, Fremont, MI 49412.

Colonial Apple Cone and baskets courtesy Country Manor, Box 520, Sperryville, VA 22740.

Miniature fruit crates and baskets courtesy The Crate Shoppe, Box 154, Kipton, OH 44049.

Quilt rack courtesy Shaker Simplicity, 4666 Quaker Trace Road, Eaton, OH 45320.

Floor tiles courtesy Hastings, 201 East 57th St., New York, NY 10022.

Dinnerware courtesy Mikasa, 30 West 23rd St., New York, NY 10010.

9

BASIC QUILTING TECHNIQUES

PATTERNS

Diagram 1 illustrates the basic sewing terms used throughout *A Patchwork Christmas*. For your convenience all the patterns are drawn full size with ¼-inch seam allowances — except for the Oven Mitt pattern on page 49 and the Christmas Stocking pattern on page 97. These two are shown one-half actual size and will need to be enlarged. Cutting and sewing lines are indicated on all patterns.

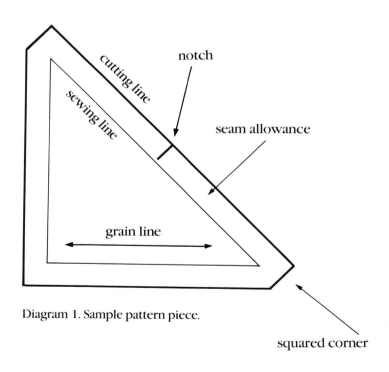

Diagram 1. Sample pattern piece.

Arrows appear on some of the pattern pieces as cutting guides. Pattern pieces with arrows should be positioned so that the arrows line up with the horizontal or vertical grain of the fabric. Patterns with straight edges but without arrows, such as squares or rectangles, should also be aligned with the vertical and horizontal grain of the fabric.

Notches are indicated on some pattern pieces. Clip notches in the fabric, where indicated, up to, but not through, the stitching line, then use them to match up edges when sewing the pieces together. Corners on triangular, diamond and odd-shaped pieces are squared to eliminate excess fabric.

Since it isn't practical to cut the patterns right out of the book, they will have to be copied in some way. The easiest method is to use a photocopying machine if one is available. Bear in mind, however, that some machines may produce copies in which the patterns are slightly reduced in size. This can create a problem later when assembling the pieces. To check the accuracy of the copies, place one of them on top of the page from which it was copied, and hold it up to the light. If there has been any change in size, ask the operator if it is possible to adjust the machine and try again.

Tracing the patterns by hand will take a little more time and care. Use a pencil, tracing paper, and a 1-inch-wide clear plastic ruler divided into $\frac{1}{8}$-inch segments for all straight lines. The plastic ruler, available in sewing and art supply stores, comes in handy when marking both the stitching lines and the cutting lines, making it quite easy to keep a constant $\frac{1}{4}$-inch distance between them. It is important to trace very carefully, as inaccurate patterns can cause a lot of problems which will show up later during the assembly process. Be sure to add the name of the design, the number of the pattern piece, and any other important markings, such as notches and arrows.

The tracing-paper pattern pieces can be used as is, by cutting them out and pinning them to the fabric, or they can be mounted on lightweight cardboard with rubber cement or spray glue available in art supply stores. When mounting the patterns, don't cut them out right after tracing them. First apply the glue, either rubber cement or spray glue, to a piece of cardboard the same size as or slightly larger than the sheet of tracing paper on which the patterns have been traced. Lay the tracing paper on top of the cardboard and smooth it down with your hand. Allow the glue to dry, then cut out all the pieces with a pair of scissors or an X-Acto knife and a steel straightedge.

A convenient way to make sturdy, long-lasting templates is to use nonslip plastic available in sewing and quilt supply stores. Trace the patterns on the plastic with a pencil as you would on tracing paper and cut them out with a pair of scissors. Template plastic is usually marked with a $\frac{1}{4}$-inch grid, which can be helpful in tracing most square or rectangular pattern pieces.

Cardboard and plastic templates are not meant to be pinned to the fabric. Lay them on the fabric one at a time, hold them in place with your hand, and trace around their edges with a pencil or water-soluble fabric marker. Hold the point of the pencil or marker right up against the edge of the pattern so that no extra seam allowance is added and the markings remain exactly the same size as the pattern.

Store the templates in an envelope marked with the name of the design. Be sure the pieces are properly marked with their piece numbers and name of the design so you can sort them out if they get mixed up with templates that belong to other designs.

FABRIC

The best fabrics for quilts are cotton and cotton blends. Most quilters prefer 100% cotton, but it isn't always available, so cotton blends can be used as well. Many fabric companies today are producing fairly extensive home sewing lines of coordinated prints and solids with quilters in mind. Machine wash and dry all cottons or cotton blends at least once before cutting to preshrink and test colorfastness. If any fabrics show a tendency to run, wash them as many times as necessary to get out all residual dye.

Silk, satin, velvet and wool also make wonderful quilts and other patchwork projects, but these fabrics are more difficult to handle than cotton. Beginners should stick to cotton until they feel ready to take on more exotic materials. Such fabrics, of course, should not be washed, but treated according to specific handling instructions pertaining to their fiber content. Because of their stretchiness and texture, knits do not work well in quilts and can greatly detract from the look of even the best-made piece.

Fabrics of different weights and textures can be mixed in a patchwork project, but remember that extra care in sewing will be required for good results since these materials may resist being stitched together evenly. Before cutting out all the pieces for an entire project, it's wise to assemble at least one quilt block as a test to see how the fabrics will behave.

It is impossible to give exact yardages for most of the designs in this book, since your own color choices will determine the necessary amounts. To help you estimate fabric requirements, a list stating how many of each pattern piece will be needed in a given color precedes the instructions for each design. When buying fabric it's always better to get a little more than you think you might need so you don't end up without enough to finish. If this does happen, however, remember that some of the most interesting quilts are those in which the colors are not exactly the same throughout, but vary somewhat from block to block, having been made with whatever fabrics were available at the time rather than yardage purchased with a particular quilt in mind.

CUTTING

Always use a pair of good, sharp scissors to cut fabric. Cutting will go more quickly if you cut through four layers of fabric at a time instead of just two. For example, if a design requires 16 pieces cut from the same pattern and the same fabric, pin and cut four times, each time cutting through four layers of fabric.

Cutting wheels are very useful for cutting out a lot of pieces with straight sides, particularly strips for strip piecing. Hold the circular blade right up against a steel or thick, plastic straightedge, apply pressure and roll the blade along the edge of the straightedge. Cutting wheels and rubber cutting mats are available through quilt supply companies and stores.

Position the patterns on the fabric so that arrows go in the same direction as the grain. Also align the sides of square or rectangular pattern pieces with the grain of the fabric. Examine the printed fabrics to determine whether the design is one-way. Most prints look fine going in any direction, but a print with a one-way pattern, particularly a stripe, should be handled carefully with the overall design of the quilt in mind.

Pin the pattern pieces in place on the fabric (unless you've mounted them on cardboard) and cut out each shape very carefully. It is extremely important to cut precisely along the cutting lines because accurate cutting will greatly affect the facility with which a design is assembled and how it will look when finished. No amount of pressing will correct puckering seams caused by inaccurate cutting. If using plastic or cardboard pattern templates, trace around them with a pencil with a sharp point or a water-soluble marker with the point held right up against the edge of the pattern. The addition of extra seam allowance that results from marking cutting lines that are even slightly larger than the pattern will cause a piece to "grow," and for a design with a lot of pieces this can become a real problem.

There is an interesting variety of marking pens and pencils in sewing and quilt supply stores. Any hard lead pencil can be used, but there are gray pencils, which leave a lighter mark, and yellow and white pencils that are good for marking dark fabrics.

Water-soluble marking pens are also useful, as the ink can be removed with a damp cloth (it is not advisable to use them for non-cotton fabrics such as wool, silk or satin). To be sure the ink is really removable, test the pen with a sample piece of fabric before marking a whole project. Be careful not to hold the pen point down in one place too long, especially when marking the quilting lines on a finished piece that has a top, batting and backing, as the ink will continue to flow into all the thicknesses, making it difficult to remove later with only a damp cloth. If there is too much ink in the fabric, washing the project will seem to be the only way to get it all out. Keep a light touch and mark quickly without sacrificing accuracy.

Chalk markers are also available in a variety of colors for marking light and dark fabrics. They are easy to use and quite accurate. Again, it is advisable to use a light touch, which I discovered marking white fabric with a blue chalk marker. My fabric was lightweight, and even though I marked the wrong side, the blue lines showed through on the right side of the quilt top. It wasn't very obvious, but you could see it if you looked closely. Most markings will wash out, but I'd rather not have to wash a project, especially a quilt, right after finishing it.

Mark fabrics with pile or a nap on the wrong side, and use a pencil or marker which make marks that won't have to be removed with water. Chalk markers that dispense a thin line of powdered chalk are probably the safest since the residue can be brushed out with the little plastic brush attached to the top of the marker.

Beginners may feel the need to mark stitching lines as well as cutting lines until sewing a ¼-inch seam becomes automatic. If this is the case, mark stitching lines on the wrong side of the fabric with a "Quilter's Quarter," a ¼-inch-wide metal or plastic sewing aid available through many quilt and sewing supply shops. Line up the edges of the Quilter's Quarter with the edge of the fabric and mark along the inside edge. Since most patchwork projects have a lot of pieces, marking the stitching lines on each piece may soon become tiresome. But it doesn't take long to become accustomed to sewing seams of a constant, even width, and you'll soon find it unnecessary to mark the stitching lines.

There are other sewing guides that will help you sew a consistent ¼-inch seam allowance. The zipper foot on my machine is just about ¼ inch in width so I use it as a guide. My machine also has a seam allowance gauge on the metal plate next to the zipper foot. If your sewing machine doesn't have a seam allowance gauge, you can use a piece of masking tape as a guide. Place it so that the edge of the tape is ¼ inch away from the needle and parallel to the side of the zipper foot. If you keep the edge of your fabric even with the edge of the tape, you will maintain a ¼-inch seam allowance.

PIECING

One of the benefits of 20th-century technology is that a quilter can choose to piece by hand or machine. You should feel free to sew whichever way is most comfortable for you. Some people believe quilts should be stitched entirely by hand. They maintain that this is the way quilts were done in the past and that the tradition should be extended to contemporary quilts as well. Others believe that if women had access to sewing machines before the middle of the last century they would certainly have used them to piece their quilts, just as they have happily used them to accomplish almost every other domestic sewing task from the middle 1800s to the present. No experienced quilter would argue that piecing is probably better done by machine. It's far stronger than hand piecing, and since the stitching in the seams doesn't show anyway, it is really overdoing it to insist that all piecing be done by hand. Too many quilts would be left unfinished, especially today, if we all tried to work by that rule. I know I would never have become a quiltmaker if I had to do all my piecing by hand.

It is true, however, that many quilts look best when the finishing — that is, the final quilting (the patterns stitched through all three layers of top, batting and back) — is done by hand. Hand quilting imparts a lovely, soft texture that is really very appealing. Even so, wonderful quilts have also been quilted to advantage by machine, so no single rule seems to apply to every patchwork project.

I use a fairly large stitch length for machine piecing, almost the largest on the machine, so that I won't have to pick at the threads too long if I have to remove the stitches to correct my work. I've also found that seams with larger stitches lie nicely and are less likely to tighten up and pucker than those with very small stitches.

For many years now I've bought cotton thread from clothing factory suppliers. They usually carry two weights, one for dresses, usually referred to as #2 cord, and a heavier one, a #3 cord, for suits and coats. I prefer the heavier weight because it's stronger. A quilt pieced and quilted with a #3 cotton cord will last a very long time. Quilting thread, available at quilting and sewing shops, also works very well.

In general, tools and materials built for industrial use are better made than those that are produced for the home consumer. This is particularly true of sewing machines. I've owned several modern home sewing machines, and because of the long hours I put in on them, the motors have burned out, or the cheap metal or plastic parts have overheated and broken. They're just not as sturdy as factory machines and they're much more expensive. A factory sewing machine is usually sold with a reconditioned, secondhand head, a new motor, and a new table. The heads are saved and reconditioned because they were originally built to last forever — and they do. Anyone who does a lot of sewing should have a sturdy machine. If you live in an apartment house and are considering buying a factory machine, remember that they are somewhat noisier than home sewing machines. If there's any question that it might disturb your neighbors, put a small carpet under it to deaden the sound.

Home sewing machines can appear more attractive because they are designed to perform many tasks. I never had any use for the embroidery stitches, or even the zigzag stitch they're so famous for. A straight seam is all a quiltmaker needs, and the embroidery stitches on a sewing machine don't begin to approach the quality of hand embroidery.

ASSEMBLY-LINE PIECING

When instructions call for the assembly of many of the same type of piece, it will save time to run each set of pieces through the machine one right after the other without stopping. After stitching the first set of pieces together, leave the presser foot down and continue stitching beyond the edges of the fabric about ½ inch to 1 inch, then feed the next piece beneath the presser foot and continue stitching. Repeat until all pieces in the step have been assembled. Clip the threads between the pieces when finished. The threads will stay twisted and keep the seams secure enough to press them open as you move on to the next step. See Diagram 2.

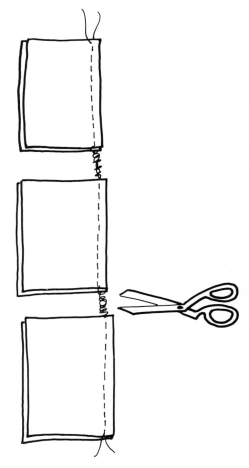

Diagram 2. Assembly-line piecing.

PRESSING

The sewing instructions for each patchwork project include frequent references to pressing seams open or, on occasion, to one side. A completed piece usually looks better when the seams have been pressed after every step, and the seams will usually lie flatter when pressed open. It is perfectly acceptable, however, to press the seams differently (and less often) if that is your personal preference. Many quilters believe a quilt will be stronger if the seams are pressed to one side, but this may or may not be true. Given the choice, I would opt for beauty rather than strength since I, for one, don't intend to subject quilts to heavy everyday use and repeated washings. Too much work and time go into each quilt for it not to be treated as a treasured object. Whether you prefer to press seams open or to one side, be careful not to stretch any of the pieces out of shape while pressing.

ENLARGING THE QUILT TOP

Quilt tops can be enlarged by adding on quilt blocks. For example, if the instructions call for twelve blocks, you can increase the overall dimensions by adding four more blocks, for a total of sixteen.

A way to increase the size of the quilt without adding more blocks is to separate the blocks you have with sashes, strips of fabric sewn between them. The sashes can be almost any width, preferably not much wider than ¼ the size of the blocks. They can be cut from fabric that is one of the colors in the blocks, or a constrasting color.

For additional width, add borders around the outside of the quilt top.

ASSEMBLING THE QUILT TOP

After the quilt top is completed, it is ready to be assembled with the batting and backing into a "quilt sandwich." The best and easiest battings to work with are those available in most sewing or quilt supply stores. Most brands are polyester, although commercial cotton batting is also available. I have never tried the cotton batting myself, but I've heard that it might not be quite as easy to quilt as the polyester batting. Cotton and wool batts, of course, were what were used in the past. They were hand-carded and carefully distributed on the backings before the quilt tops were placed on top and basted. The reason for quilting the three layers together in the first place was to keep the batting in place. The closer the lines of quilting were to each other, the less likely it was that the batting, which was loose, would bunch up and move around. Today's commercial battings are wonderful because there is virtually no danger of this happening, which renders extensive quilting unnecessary unless desired.

Commercial battings come in several weights: regular, low-loft and high-loft. The thinner the batting, the easier it will be to produce small stitches, so for very fine work, the low-loft is best. The regular weight is fine for almost any project, and the high-loft is good for nice, plump comforters or tied quilts. Because the high-loft battings are much thicker than the others, they are not suitable for fine quilting. Each weight is available in several sizes, from small sizes for small projects, such as baby quilts, to king-size quilts.

Most quilts have white, or a light-colored fabric for the backing, since most quilting is done with white thread. Some are backed with fabric in one of the colors in the pieced top. Others are backed with a contrasting fabric. Any of these choices is purely a matter of personal preference, but there are a few things to keep in mind: It's not a good idea to use a dark fabric for the backing if the quilt top is of a light color, particularly if the batting is thin. The backing will show through and give the quilt top a "dirty" look.

If the color of the quilting thread contrasts strongly with the top or the backing, extra care should be taken to keep the stitches regular in size. Uneven stitches will be much more obvious on a contrasting color.

Most cotton and cotton blend fabrics are 45 to 48 inches wide. Some are still 36 inches wide. When buying yardage for a backing, it will be necessary to figure out how much the project will require if it is larger than the width of the fabric. It may take two or more lengths pieced together to accommodate the size of the project. For example, if a quilt measures 90 × 90 inches, it will require two 2½-yard lengths of 48-inch fabric, or a total of 5 yards for the backing.

To assemble the quilt top, batting and backing, spread the backing wrong side up on the floor, on a low-pile carpet if possible. The nap on the carpet will keep the fabric from slipping around, making it much easier to work with. If a carpet isn't available, tape the edges of the fabric to the floor with masking tape to keep the back from slipping around beneath the batting and quilt top.

Place the batting on top of the back and smooth it out. Stretch the batting slightly to ease out the slack, but not too much. Now place the quilt top right side up on top of the batting and carefully smooth it out until it looks square and free of any puckering or pulling.

Working from the center of the quilt out toward the edges, pin all three layers together (without catching pins in the carpet). Insert pins at least every foot or so, also along the edges. Pick up the quilt, turn it over and straighten it out face down on the floor; check to see that the back hasn't moved during pinning. If it has, turn the quilt over and repin where necessary until all layers are smooth and straight.

Baste all three layers together by hand, starting from the center and basting horizontally out toward the sides. Baste horizontal rows, working down toward the bottom, then up to the top. Then baste vertical rows from top to bottom. When all the basting is finished, machine-stitch around entire perimeter of the quilt top, ¼ inch from the edge. This stay-stitching will hold the edges firmly in place during the quilting process and make it easier to attach the quilt to the quilting frame, if you use one.

THE FRAME

Quilts can be quilted without a frame and they often are, but those that have been quilted in a frame have an especially smooth, flat appearance. It might be difficult at first to get used to quilting with a frame, because the sewing surface is taut and seems to resist flexing as the needle is pushed up and down through the quilt in a running stitch. After a while, however, most quilters come to prefer it and even find it easier, especially since the results are so pleasing.

Different frames will have different instructions for attaching the quilts, but usually a cloth tape is stapled to each of the cross bars, and the top and bottom edges of the quilt are then basted to these tapes. Stretch the edge of the quilt a bit when basting it to the tape. Make sure the top and bottom edges of the quilt are directly in line with each other so there is no diagonal pulling when they are rolled up.

When the top and bottom edges are fixed in the frame, roll the quilt up tightly from both ends until the center is exposed in the middle and tightly stretched. Lace the sides of the quilt to the side pieces of the frame with needle and thread, or use a length of cloth tape, depending on how the frame is constructed. The idea is to get the quilt firmly and evenly stretched throughout, because once quilted it will retain the shape it has been given from being stretched in the frame. I pull the quilt taut so there is no sagging in the middle and so it bounces back up if pressed down. See Diagram 3.

Quilt frames are available through suppliers that advertise regularly in quilting magazines. Some suppliers carry more than one type. There are single-project standing frames, smaller than the one described above, designed for quilting small projects and single blocks. Blocks can be quilted one at a time and assembled after they are finished.

Hoops such as lap hoops, standing hoops, and standing hoops with universal ball joints, like the one pictured on page 159, allow the work to be turned at any angle. (See Source List on page 9 for merchandise information.) The quilt

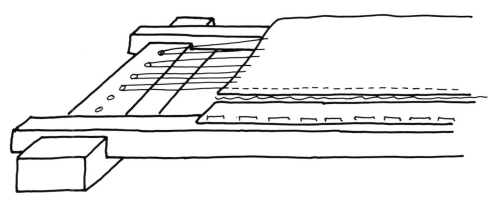

Diagram 3. Baste quilt to tape. Roll up and stretch tightly. Lash sides to side pieces.

20

is first spread out on top of the inner ring. Then the outer ring is placed on top of the quilt and forced down over the inner ring, tightly stretching the quilt. The set screw on the outer ring is then tightened to hold the quilt rigidly in place.

Hoops work very well and are especially useful to people who don't have room for a floor frame. For most quilted projects it will be necessary to machine-baste fabric extenders about 18 inches wide to each side. This gives the hoop something to grab on to so the corners and borders of the quilt can be stretched and exposed for quilting on the inside of the hoop.

QUILTING

Once it is stretched, the quilt is ready to mark. There is a variety of marking pens and pencils for quilts.

Since you will be marking the quilting designs on the right side of the fabric, the marks should be as light as possible, but still visible enough to work without straining your eyes. Make your selection according to whether you intend to wash or dry-clean the finished quilt to remove the marks. Some quilters don't have to do either, since the marks they make are so light they virtually disappear during the quilting process. The quilt designs can be drawn on the fabric with the aid of a ruler, or using commercial or homemade stencils. You can make your own stencils by drawing on lightweight cardboard and cutting out the designs with an X-Acto knife. Stencil cutting kits containing electric hot pens and a roll of plastic are advertised in quilt magazines and are probably available in sewing and quilt supply stores.

One of the simplest and most common ways to mark a quilt is with "outline" quilting. Whatever the motif, you can quilt around it $\frac{1}{4}$ inch away from its edge, using a Quilter's Quarter as a guide, or a transparent ruler that shows $\frac{1}{4}$-inch segments. Quilting around the outside of each shape in this manner is always quite pleasing. It is also the basis of Hawaiian-style quilting, in which not only the motif is outlined, but each line of quilting is outlined by another, and another, radiating outward until every inch is quilted.

You can use a square grid pattern for quilting, which you can draw diagonally, or vertically and horizontally across the quilt.

Masking tape can also be used as a stitch guide and is available in several widths. Choose the width that will be the same as the distance you want between the stitching lines. Position a strip of tape on the quilt and quilt along one side using the edge as a guide. Remove the tape and reposition it (or a fresh piece) on one side of the quilting line. Quilt another line along the edge of the tape. Repeat the process until all the quilting lines going in that direction are finished. Position a strip of tape at right angles to the other lines and repeat until all the quilting is finished.

The traditional way to quilt is with one hand holding the needle over the surface of the quilt, and the other positioned underneath to feel the needle as it comes through the fabric and direct it back up to the top. It is best to protect both the finger that pushes the needle through and the one underneath with some sort of finger guard, such as a thimble or leather finger guard (both are sold in most quilt supply stores). Quilters have different preferences, so it is entirely a matter of choice as to which one you select. I use a thimble with a ridge around the top that keeps the needle from slipping off the tip of my finger. I still haven't found a finger guard I'm really happy with for my other hand. I sometimes quilt without any at all, which isn't so good since the needle digs at my fingers a bit.

Quilting is easiest with a fairly short needle. The thinner the needle, the more easily it will pass through the fabric. Don't choose a needle so thin that the eye is too small for the thread.

To keep the thread from twisting too much and knotting up, pull it through a piece of beeswax (this also seems to make the thread stronger). Tie a knot in the end of the thread, insert the needle through the top layer of the quilt about an inch away from where you want to start quilting. Pull the needle up and through the fabric at the point where you want to start — right up to the knot. Pull gently at the knot until it pops through the top layer. The knot will now be concealed between the quilt top and backing. Knots should never show on the front or back of the quilt. See Diagram 4.

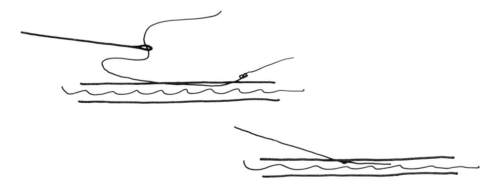

Diagram 4. Insert needle between layers. Pull knot through to inside.

The way the actual quilting is done is also a matter of preference. You will have to experiment to discover the quilting technique that is most comfortable for you. It is generally agreed that a series of running stitches — at least two to four — is better than quilting a stitch at a time. A series of running stitches usually produces a straighter line than the single-stitch method. Make the stitches as even and as small as you can. It is thought by some, and I think unfairly, that there should be as many as 11, even up to 13, stitches per inch. I've seen a number of lovely quilts in which the stitches were by no means small. My stitches are generally 10 to the inch, depending on how thick the fabric and batting are. If the stitches are too small, they become hard to see, and not as pretty, in my opinion, as a clearly visible line of even stitches. If you plan on entering your quilts in shows and contests you will find that small stitch size is a very important part of the judging. By observing the work of other quilters, you can get some ideas on how to improve your own stitching technique and speed.

To finish a line of quilting, wind the thread around the needle two or three times just where it comes up at the surface of the quilt. Pull the needle through to make a knot at this point. Insert the needle just one stitch length beyond this point between the two layers of the quilt. Bring the needle up about 1 inch away and pull the knot through so it lies between the two layers. Pull the thread and clip it off at the point where it comes up through the fabric. The end of the thread will disappear between the layers. See Diagram 5.

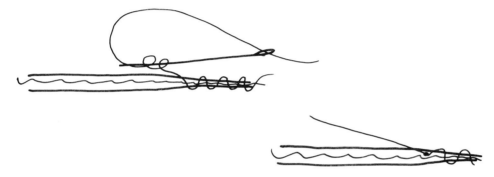

Diagram 5. Wrap thread around needle to make knot. Pull knot through to inside. Push needle up and clip thread.

Quilting can also be done by machine. The quilt is prepared in the same way — all three layers are basted together as for quilting by hand — and inserted under the presser foot. The only disadvantage is that larger quilts can be very cumbersome and hard to handle while guiding them through the machine, especially when there are a lot of curves. It might be wiser when planning a large piece to think about quilting a block at a time and assembling them afterwards. Great care must be taken to make sure that the quilt top and backing feed through the machine at the same rate so that they don't pull away from each other and pucker. It might help to stretch the quilt firmly while sewing (gently when sewing on the bias); your right hand in front of the presser foot and your left hand behind it. Very pleasing results are possible with machine piecing as long as all layers remain smooth and flat without pulling away from each other in different directions. To make knots at each end of a line of quilting, backstitch over the first stitch and last stitches.

BINDING THE QUILT

Once the quilting is finished, the quilt can be removed from the frame. The edges then need to be finished with a binding, which can be of any size. It can be a self binding, the same color as the overall color of the quilt, or a contrasting color. The following instructions are for making a ½-inch-wide binding for a low-loft quilt.

A binding with a ½-inch finished width on a low-loft quilt requires 2-inch-wide strips of fabric cut on the bias or on the straight of the goods. The advantage of a bias binding is that it is more flexible and can be shaped around curved edges. Cut along the vertical or horizontal grain of the fabric for strips cut on the straight. To prepare the strips for a bias binding, fold over one end of a rectangle of fabric on a diagonal so that the cut edge of the fabric is even with the selvage edge. See Diagram 6.

Press a crease along this fold, which is the true bias of the fabric. Unfold fabric and mark off the fabric in 2-inch-wide diagonal strips, using the crease as the first line. See Diagram 7.

Cut as many bias strips as needed to go around the perimeter of the quilt and stitch the ends together. Press seams open. See Diagram 8.

Another, even faster way to cut large quantities of bias trim is to begin with a rectangle of fabric twice as long as it is wide. Mark diagonal cutting lines as described above. Then cut off the triangles left over at each end and set them

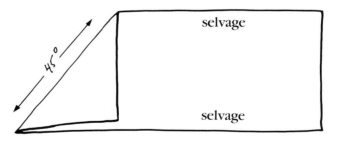

Diagram 6. Fold fabric on the diagonal.

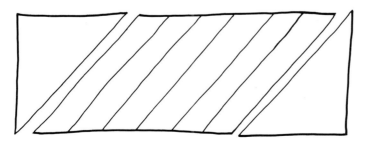

Diagram 7. Cut 2-inch-wide diagonal strips.

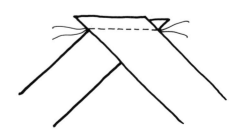

Diagram 8. Stitch strips together, end to end.

24

aside. Now, with right sides facing, pin edges of the fabric together, staggering strips so that the bottom ends move over one place, as shown. Machine-stitch the edges together in this position to make a tube. Starting at one end of the tube, cut out one continuous bias strip. See Diagram 9.

If you like, the completed binding strip can be preshaped before attaching it to the quilt by folding and pressing it in half first, and then folding the sides in to the middle and pressing again. This can be accomplished even more easily with a tape pressing aid, a simple gadget available in most quilt and fabric shops. See Diagram 10.

Attach binding to quilt in the middle of one side, not at a corner. Fold under one short end of binding, then pin binding along one edge on top side of the quilt, matching raw edge of binding to raw edge of quilt. Using a ½-inch seam allowance, stitch along binding to within ½ inch of the corner and then backstitch. Lift presser foot, remove quilt, and clip threads. See Diagram 11.

Fold binding up at a 45-degree angle, crease with finger and pin. See Diagram 12.

Fold binding down to form ½-inch tuck, insert needle exactly at point where first stitch line ended, lower presser foot and continue sewing. Sew a few inches, remove and check to see that the corner will fold neatly with just the right amount of binding and adjust if necessary before continuing on to the other corners. See Diagram 13.

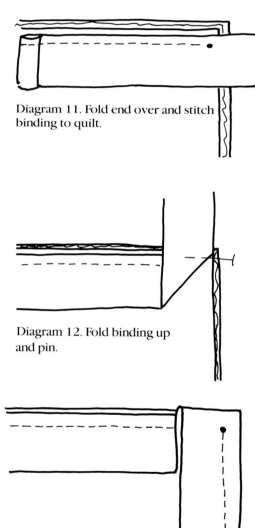

Diagram 11. Fold end over and stitch binding to quilt.

Diagram 12. Fold binding up and pin.

Diagram 13. Fold binding down at corner.

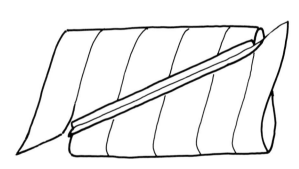

Diagram 9. Cut tube of fabric into one continuous bias strip.

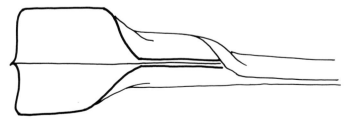

Diagram 10. Preshaping bias binding.

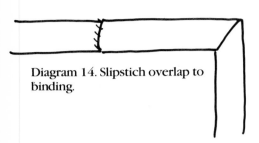

Diagram 14. Slipstich overlap to binding.

To finish binding, continue sewing about an inch beyond starting point and trim. Fold binding over to other side of quilt. Turn edge under and pin, folding and mitering the corners. Slipstitch binding by hand. See Diagram 14.

A very nice finishing touch for any handmade project would be your signature embroidered on the lower right-hand border, or anywhere it can be seen. If you plan on showing it in public, it's always wise to add the year it was made and a copyright symbol, a c inside a circle. This will help protect your design. I usually embroider my name, the date and copyright symbol in thread that is the same color as the fabric on which it is stitched. This makes the information visible, but not intrusive. At other times, I use a contrasting color, depending on what seems right for the overall design. Other information, such as the name of the town or city in which you live, the person or purpose you made it for, which could later be of personal or historic interest, can also be embroidered on the quilt top, or on the back if you feel this much information on the front of the quilt would be too distracting.

HANGING AND DISPLAYING QUILTS

When displaying quilts on beds or on the wall there are a few things that should be kept in mind. Quilts should be kept out of direct sunlight which will cause the colors to fade over a period of time. Drawing the curtains or blinds when the room in which a quilt is displayed is not in use will be helpful in cutting down the time it will be exposed to light. Quilts should also be protected from extreme changes in temperature and humidity.

There are several ways to hang quilts which will minimize the strain their weight will put on threads and fibers. They should never be suspended with nails, staples, tacks, or even pushpins. One way to hang a quilt is from a pole inserted through a muslin sleeve which is attached to the wrong side of the quilt across the top. The sleeve should be wide enough so the pole can be easily inserted. Baste through all three thickness of the quilt at the top and bottom edges of the sleeve. Insert the pole at either end of the sleeve and attach it to the wall.

Another way is to use a strip of Velcro about two inches wide and the length of the top of the quilt. Baste the soft side of the Velcro strip across the top of the quilt (or whichever side you wish to hang it from). Staple the other side of the strip to a flat board attached to the wall. To hang the quilt, stretch the top of the quilt slightly when attaching the two strips of Velcro to each other. Quilts can be easily removed and rotated with this method.

The safest way of all to hang a quilt is to baste it to a sheet stretched tightly over a wood frame. To relieve the quilt from the strain of its weight as much as possible, baste it to the sheet around all four sides and throughout the entire surface in vertical and horizontal rows. Then hang the frame on the wall as you would a large picture frame.

Quilts should not be displayed for indefinite periods of time. They'll need a rest from vertical hanging and from the obvious wear and tear they'll take if they're spread out on beds. They'll also need a break from light once in a while. In addition, if you have several quilts and can rotate them, you will welcome the visual change. If artwork of any kind remains in the same place for a long period of time we get so used to it we don't see it any more.

CARE OF QUILTS

Because modern commercial batting is so well made, it can be washed easily without bunching up or shifting between the lines of quilting. As long as the fabrics are preshrunk and colorfast, there's no reason a quilt can't be washed by hand using a very mild detergent. It's not a good idea, however, to wash quilts by machine, because the stress of the machine's agitating action causes a lot more wear and tear than washing by hand. Hand washing is probably easiest in a bathtub or large sink. Never scrub or rub layers together. Gently press the water through the quilt. Drain the water, refill the tub and repeat the process until the water remains clear. Then drain the water off for the last time, press out as much of it as possible, and gently blot with towels. Lay the quilt out flat to dry. If it is to be laid to dry outside, be sure it is kept out of direct sunlight which can fade the colors. Do not hang a wet quilt on a clothesline. The excess weight will put a great deal of stress on the fabric and stitching. Cotton, or cotton blend quilts can be dry cleaned, but after a while they don't look quite as bright and clean as they do when they're hand washed.

Antique quilts, of course, must be handled with very special care. It is best to discuss the care they require with an antique dealer or an expert in textile conservation.

All quilts, new or old, should be folded in acid-free tissue paper and stored in acid-free cardboard boxes. See that they are clean and free from dirt which invites pests to eat right through the fabric to get to food. Never store them in plastic bags, especially for long periods of time. They will be deprived of air circulation and exposed to chemicals which may be harmful to the fibers. There is also a danger that moisture might be trapped inside which could cause mildew. If they are to be stored on wood shelves, or in drawers or trunks (even cedar) protect them from the acids in the wood with clean muslin or acid-free tissue. Some quilters make cotton sleeves that resemble large pillow cases for each quilt. Refold your quilts every six months so the folds fall in different places with crumpled tissue paper in each fold to prevent permanent creasing.

Quilts are meant to be used, if not on beds, then displayed where they can be seen and appreciated. Any quilt will age in time, but if properly cared for, it can be enjoyed for generations.

MAKING PILLOWS

Making a patchwork pillow top is a nice way for a beginner to become acquainted with various quiltmaking techniques without feeling over-whelmed by a big project. An experienced quiltmaker can experiment with a quilt block pattern before deciding definitely to use it and never have to feel that it will go to waste if it doesn't end up in a quilt. Patchwork blocks made into pillows are wonderful gifts that require a manageable amount of work. How intricate the designs become is entirely up to you.

In this section there are instructions for finishing pillow tops with ruffles, cord edges and binding, and assembling them with various types of closures. But first, here are a few hints on creating colorful and dramatic pillow tops just by attaching ribbons and lace to a square of fabric.

PILLOWS WITH RIBBONS AND LACE

You can start with a square of any size. Those shown here are for 12- and 14-inch pillow forms.

MATERIALS

Fabric for pillow tops and backs measuring 12½ or 14½ inches

7- or 8-inch square of fabric of contrasting color for center square (optional)

1 yard of ribbon and/or lace for each pillow top

2 yards of 5- or 10-inch-wide strips of fabric for ruffle (optional) or

1⅔ yards of 2-inch-wide fabric for binding edge (optional)

SEWING INSTRUCTIONS

Draw a 14½- or 12½-inch square on a sheet of tracing paper. On the 14½-inch square, mark an 8-inch square inside it 3¼ inches in from the outside edge. On the 12½-inch square, mark a 7-inch square inside it 2¾ inches in from the outside edge. Cut out the inner squares neatly and use them to cut small squares. See Diagram 1.

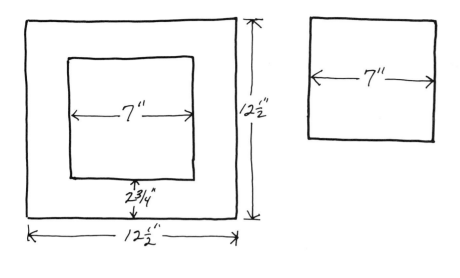

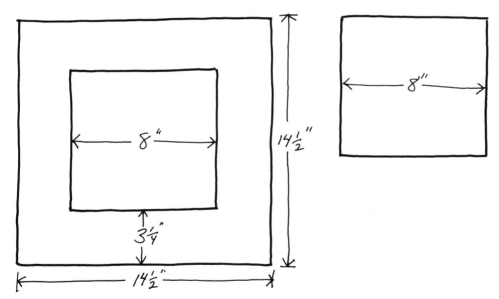

Diagram 1. Cut out patterns.

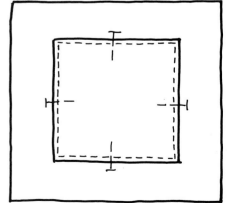

Diagram 2. Pin and stitch center square.

Using the paper patterns, cut the larger squares from fabric you wish to use for the pillow tops. On the large square, mark the inside square on the fabric with a pencil. Use this line as a guide to apply fabric for the center square and the lace and ribbon trim.

To apply the center square of a contrasting color, pin and stitch it to the pillow top around the outside edge. See Diagram 2.

Diagram 3. Make pleat at corner.

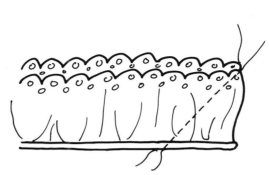

Diagram 4. Fold lace and stitch seam at a 45-degree angle.

Diagram 5. Wide lace with mitered corners.

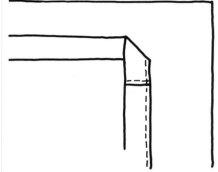

Diagram 6. Turn last corner, cut ribbon, turn end under and stitch.

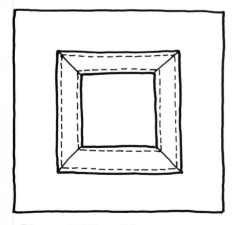

Diagram 7. Miter ribbons at corners. Stitch around inside edge.

Lace Trim

To apply lace, start on one side (not at a corner) of the inside square marked with pencil, or the fabric center square. Sew lace to pillow top, finished side facing out. Stitch to corner; make a small pleat so lace can turn corner. See Diagram 3.

Continue sewing and repeat at each corner. To finish, stitch lace ¼ inch beyond first end, cut lace, turn end under ¼ inch and stitch.

To make mitered corners for wide lace, fold lace right sides in and stitch a seam at a 45-degree angle at least 10 inches from one end of lace for an 8-inch inside square, and at least 9 inches from end of lace for a 7-inch inside square. Trim lace to within ¼ inch of seam. Press seam open. See Diagram 4.

Fold and stitch other corners in the same way, leaving 7 or 8 inches respectively between seam at one corner and seam at next corner. Pin and stitch lace to pillow top following inside square. See Diagram 5.

Ribbon Trim

Ribbon can be used alone or to cover raw edges of lace trim. Starting ¼ inch in from one corner, sew ribbon around outside edge of inside square just outside the stitch line. Stop with needle down at next corner, turn pillow top, turn ribbon around corner and continue sewing. Repeat at each corner. Turn last corner and cut ribbon off, leaving about 1 inch to turn edge under. Fold end under and stitch down over other end. See Diagram 6.

Fold the ribbon neatly at each corner to make mitered corners. Pin and stitch in place around inside edge. See Diagram 7.

To finish pillow with ruffle or other types of finishes, refer to the instructions that follow.

ASSEMBLING THE PILLOW TOP

Once you have completed a patchwork pillow top, you will also need to cut a piece of matching or contrasting fabric the same size as the finished pillow top for the pillow back, plus a piece of white fabric to line the patchwork top, and a piece of batting to give it body (the batting is optional).

Spread out the white lining, smooth the batting on top of the lining and lay the pillow top on top of the batting, right side up. Pin all three layers together and machine-baste ⅛ inch all around the outside edge. The layer of batting adds a soft, plump appearance to the pillow top, but it is not essential and can be omitted if you don't plan to quilt the pillow top. If you wish to quilt the design, however, use a layer of batting to lend dimension to your stitches. Any quilting — by hand or machine — should be done at this point.

EDGE FINISHING

Doubled Ruffle

To make a 2-inch-wide doubled ruffle, cut four 5-inch-wide strips that are 1½ to 2 times the length of one side of the finished pillow top, depending on how full you want the gathered ruffle to be. For example, if the pillow is a 10-inch square, cut four 5 × 15-, or four 5 × 20-inch fabric strips. Or simply cut and piece a 5-inch-wide strip that measures 1½ to 2 times the perimeter of the pillow top. One-third yard of 44-inch-wide fabric will yield enough 5-inch-wide strips to make a generous doubled ruffle for a 10-, 12-, or even a 14-inch square pillow.

Sew the strips together end to end and press seams open. After sewing the ends together to make one continuous loop, fold the ruffle in half lengthwise, right side out. Match raw edges, and press fold in ruffle. Machine-baste through both thicknesses ⅛ inch from raw edges all around the ruffle. Add a second row of stitching all around, ⅛ inch away from the first, starting and stopping at the same place. Pull both threads in both rows of stitching at the same time to gather the ruffle.

Pin ruffle to outside edge of the pillow top (folded edge of ruffle facing in). If using a ruffle composed of four equal pieces, the seam lines should be positioned at each corner, or at the center sides of the pillow top. This helps in judging how much ruffle should be distributed along each side of the pillow when adjusting gathers on the ruffle. If using a randomly pieced ruffle, fold it in fourths and clip a notch in the center edge at each fold to use as placement guides. Adjust gathers so they're evenly distributed on each side with more gathers at the corners so the ruffle will turn corners gracefully.

Sew ruffle to pillow top just inside lines of gathers. See Diagram 8.

Single Ruffle

A ruffle of a single thickness can be made in the same way as the Doubled Ruffle above, except that the outer edge must be finished either with a hem or with lace trim.

For a 2-inch-wide single ruffle, cut 3-inch-wide strips in the lengths described above for Doubled Ruffle. Fold one long edge over twice and stitch a ¼-inch hem along the entire edge. Add two lines of machine basting along the other edge for gathering and proceed as for Doubled Ruffle. A row of lace edging can also be added if you choose. On some laces, both edges are finished. For others it will be necessary to tuck the raw edge of the lace into the edge of the ruffle before hemming. See Diagram 9.

Cord Edge

Cut enough fabric for about 1¼ yards of 2-inch bias strip and assemble according to instructions for Binding the Quilt, page 24. Replace presser foot with a zipper foot. Fold bias strip over 1¼-yard length of cord. Making sure edges of bias strip remain even, stitch close to cord. Overlapping ends of cord in the middle of one side, pin and stitch cord to outside edge of right side of pillow top. To turn corners, clip seam allowance of binding at corners up to but not through stitch line. To finish, follow instructions for Assembling the Pillow Front and Back. See Diagram 10.

Knife Edge with Binding

One of the simplest and nicest ways to finish a pillow is to bind it as you would a quilt. Pin and stitch the pillow top to the pillow back, wrong sides facing, leaving one side open. Cut and apply the binding following instructions for Binding the Quilt, page 24. Insert the pillow form and close the opening by hand or machine.

ASSEMBLING THE PILLOW FRONT AND BACK

The following instructions are for three types of pillow closures: simple closure by hand, overlapped fabric back, and a lapped zipper. All provide for a ½-inch seam allowance.

Closure by Hand

With right sides facing, pin pillow back to pillow top. Keep ruffle, if used, tucked in toward center. Starting about 1 inch before corner on one side, sew top to back around three sides, ending about 1 inch past corner on fourth side. Leave the remainder of the fourth unstitched for turning. Stitching around

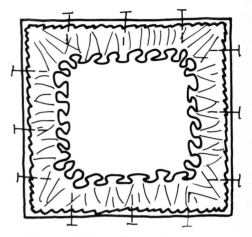

Diagram 8. Pin ruffle to pillow top.

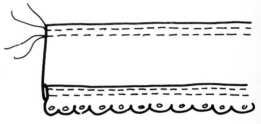

Diagram 9. Add lace edging to single ruffle.

Diagram 10. Overlap ends of cord.

both corners on the fourth side makes it easier to close the opening after turning and stuffing the pillow.

Clip corners and turn the pillow right side out. Insert pillow form, pin opening and whipstitch closed by hand. To wash, clip hand-stitching, and remove the pillow form.

Overlapped Fabric Back

For an overlapped pillow closure, you will need to cut two pieces instead of one for the pillow back. Cut each piece 1 inch longer than the width of the pillow × 2½ inches longer than half the length of the finished pillow. For a 10-inch-square pillow, for example: cut two 11 × 7½-inch pieces. Stitch a ¼-inch hem in one long side of each piece. Now lay one piece over the other so that together they measure 11 × 11 inches with the hemmed edges overlapping in the center. Machine-baste the pieces together at sides where edges overlap. With right sides facing, lay pieced back on pillow top and pin in place (keep ruffle, if used, tucked in toward center of pillow). Stitch around all four sides. Clip corners and turn. Pillow is inserted through opening where the two back pieces overlap. See Diagram 11.

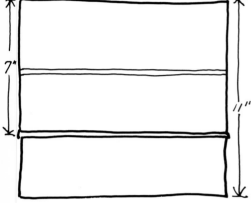

Diagram 11. Overlap two back pieces.

Lapped Zipper

Select a zipper that is 2 inches shorter than finished pillow size. For example, if finished pillow measures 12 inches, buy a 10-inch zipper.

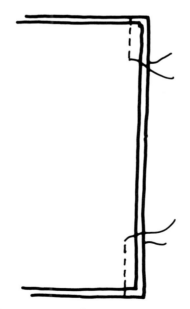

Diagram 12. Stitch one inch in from seamline on each end of one side.

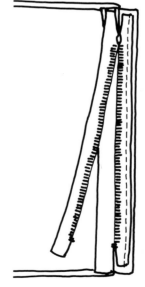

Diagram 13. Stitch one side of zipper to pillow front seam allowance.

With right sides of pillow front and back facing, stitch them together 1 inch from each end on one side; backstitch for strength. Press seam open along entire length of side. See Diagram 12.

Replace presser foot with zipper foot. With wrong side of back facing up, fold out the seam allowance of the pillow top. Place the unzipped zipper face down with teeth on center seam line (zipper tab and stop should be at points where stitching ends). Stitch down the length of the zipper, ¼ inch from teeth, sewing through pillow front seam allowance. See Diagram 13.

Close zipper, turn it face up and smooth seam allowance away from zipper. Topstitch down length of zipper through seam allowance about ⅛ inch from seam near zipper teeth. See Diagram 14.

Spread open front and back of pillow, turn zipper face down on the seam. Starting at top of zipper, stitch across the seam from pillow front to pillow back, turn corner and stitch zipper tape to pillow back down the length of the zipper. Turn corner at the other end and stitch across from back to front. See Diagram 15.

With right sides facing, pin pillow front and back together around three remaining sides. Be sure to open the zipper a few inches after pinning sides so that the pillow isn't sewn shut with the zipper closed. Sew front to back around three sides, starting and stopping just above the tab, and stop at head and foot of zipper. Clip corners, trim seams and turn the pillow right side out. Insert pillow form and zip closed. See Diagram 16.

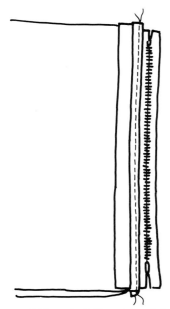

Diagram 14. Topstitch first side of zipper in place.

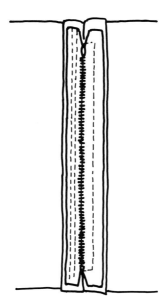

Diagram 15. Stitch remaining side of zipper in place.

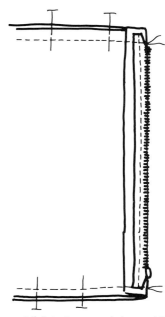

Diagram 16. Stitch around three sides of pillow.

CHRISTMAS TREE BORDER

The Christmas Tree Border is a simple, yet versatile design that can dress up any number of homemade gifts or ready-made items. The instructions below are for a border of eight trees for a 20-inch-square napkin. Add or subtract trees as necessary for napkins of different sizes, or to make borders for towels, tablecloths, aprons, curtains, etc. Just vary the number of trees to suit the dimensions of each item.

Detail of Border.

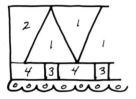

Piecing diagram.

Table Linens

MATERIALS

To make a border strip approximately 4 inches deep and 20 inches (8 trees) wide, you will need the following materials:

Fabric

Pattern piece	Number of pieces
1	4 red, 4 green, 7 white
2	2 white (cut one, flop pattern and cut another)
3	4 red, 4 green
4	9 white
5	4 white, red, or green (for corners of tablecloths, etc.)

Other Materials
21 inches of 1-inch ungathered cotton lace

SEWING INSTRUCTIONS

To make the treetops, sew one white piece #1 to the right-hand side of each of seven green and red triangles (#1), matching the notches. Right sides together, stitch one white piece #2 to the right-hand side of the eighth red or green triangle, matching the notches. See Diagram 1. Press the seams open on each pair.

Sew the treetops (all the pairs of #1 pieces) together in a row, matching the notches and alternating red and green. Sew the remaining white #2 piece to the left-hand edge of the strip of treetops. Press the seams open and set the strip aside.

To make the tree trunks, sew a white #4 piece to the right-hand side of each of eight red and green #3 pieces. Press the seams open. Stitch the tree trunks (#3 and #4 pieces) together in a row, alternating red and green trunks to match the order of colors in the strip of treetops. Sew the remaining white #4 piece to the left-hand end of the strip. Press the seams open.

Sew the row of treetops to the row of tree trunks so that each trunk lines up under the center of a treetop of the same color. See Diagram 2. Press the seam up toward the treetops.

Sew a length of 1-inch-wide cotton lace along the bottom edge of the tree trunks, right sides together. See Diagram 3. Press the seam up toward the trees, away from the lace.

Diagram 1. Stitch white triangle (#1) to seven of the red and green triangles (#1); stitch a white #2 to last triangle.

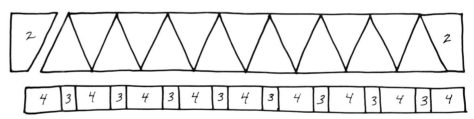

Diagram 2. Assemble strip of tree trunks.

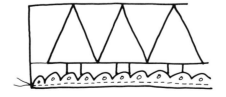

Diagram 3. Sew lace trim to bottom of tree strip.

Place the completed border strip facedown on one edge of the napkin with the pointed ends of the treetops positioned about 5 inches from the edge of the napkin. Sew the border to the napkin along the treetop side. See Diagram 4. The ends of the border strip should extend approximately ¼ inch beyond the edges of the napkin (trim the ends of the border strip if necessary) so that they can be turned under later and hemmed.

Turn the border faceup, pin the bottom edge in place and press. Turn the ends of the border under so that they are flush with the side edges of the napkin. Pin in place. See Diagram 5. Using a cording foot, machine-stitch the bottom edge of the border to the napkin along the lace edge, sewing as close to the trees as possible. Whipstitch the ends of the border in place by hand.

Give the finished napkin a final pressing.

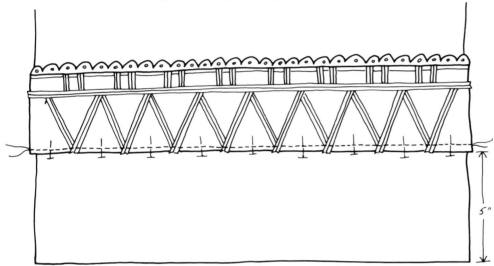

Diagram 4. With right sides facing, stitch border to napkin.

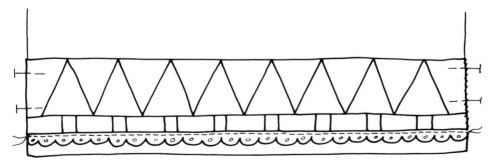

Diagram 5. Fold border strip down, fold ends under, stitch in place.

Corners and Four-sided Borders

Make four rows of trees as described above. Before adding the lace trim, sew a white, red, or green square (pattern piece #5) to the left end of each of the four rows of trees. Treat the square as part of the border.

Starting at the upper left-hand corner of the square (piece #5), add the lace trim to each border strip. Make a small pleat at the corner and turn the corner at the lower left of the square (piece #5). See Diagram 6.

Place the first border strip facedown along one side of the tablecloth, with the treetops about 5 inches from the edge and the corner. Sew the border strip to the tablecloth along the treetop side. Then turn, press and stitch down the lace edge of the strip as for the napkin.

Position the next border strip at a right angle to the first, so that the square (#5) starts at the arrow as shown. See Diagram 7. The top edge of the second border strip should lap over the right end of the first border strip. Repeat for each corner.

To finish, turn under the loose end of the fourth corner square (piece #5) and whipstitch by hand.

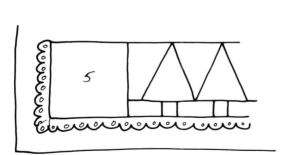

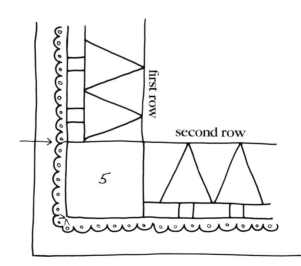

Diagram 6. Sew corner square (#5) to left end of strip. Add lace trim.

Diagram 7. Position second border strip at right angles to first.

Oven Mitt

Cut from pre-quilted fabric, this Oven Mitt is very easy to make.

MATERIALS

⅓ **yard of pre-quilted fabric**
1½ **inches of ¼-inch ribbon for loop**
½ **yard of 2-inch bias trim for ½-inch-wide**
   binding

SEWING INSTRUCTIONS

The Oven Mitt pattern is shown at one-half actual size. To enlarge the pattern, draw a grid of 1-inch squares (or use purchased graph paper). Copy the pattern onto the grid and cut it out from paper or lightweight cardboard.

Cut two oven mitt shapes (one right and one left) from the pre-quilted fabric.

Piece together a two-tree-wide Christmas Tree Border and sew the top edge of the border to the mitt front about ⅜ inch from the wrist edge. Either piece can be used as the mitt front, depending on whether you want to make a right-handed or left-handed mitt. Stitch the bottom edge of the border to the mitt just below the tree trunks. See Diagram 1.

With right sides together, pin and stitch the mitt front to the mitt back. Sew all around the outside edge, leaving the wrist edge open. Trim the curves and turn the mitt right side out.

Pin and sew a loop of ¼-inch ribbon to the top edge of the seam on the thumb side of the mitt.

Fold over one end of the strip of bias binding about ½ inch and pin the binding to the right side of the wrist edge of the mitt. See Diagram 2. Using a ½-inch seam allowance, sew the binding around the wrist edge of the mitt, ending ½ inch beyond the folded end. Trim the binding.

Fold the binding over to the inside of the mitt, turn under the raw edge ½ inch and pin around the entire inside edge. Whipstitch the binding to the inside of the mitt by hand to finish.

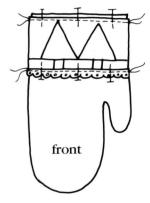

Diagram 1. Stitch Christmas Tree Border to front of Oven Mitt.

Diagram 2. Pin and stitch hanging loop and bias trim to top edge of Mitt.

Potholder

The tree shapes that make up the Christmas Tree Border can be assembled to rotate around a central point, creating an octagonal design within an 8-inch square.

MATERIALS

Fabric

Pattern piece	Number of pieces
1	4 red (or light green); 4 green
3	4 red (or light green); 4 green
4A	16 white
6	4 white, red, or green

8½-inch square of red or green fabric for the back

Other Materials

8½-inch square of batting

1 yard of 2-inch bias trim to make ½-inch binding for the outside edge

1½ inches of ¼-inch red or green ribbon for loop

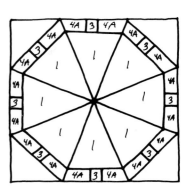

Piecing diagram.

SEWING INSTRUCTIONS

Sew one white piece #4A to each side of each piece #3. Press the seams open.

Sew one piece #1 (red, light green, or green) to the top of each 4A-3-4A section you have just completed to make one tree. See Diagram 1. Press the seams open.

Sew two trees of contrasting colors together side-by-side. See Diagram 2. Repeat for four pairs of trees.

Sew two pairs of trees together. See Diagram 3. Repeat to make two sets of four trees each. Press the seams open.

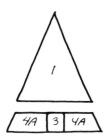

Diagram 1. Sew trunk section to treetop.

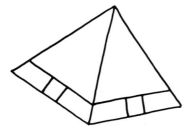

Diagram 2. Sew two trees together to make a pair.

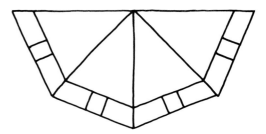

Diagram 3. Sew two pairs of trees together to make one half octagon.

Sew the two sets (halves of an octagon) together along the straight edge, matching the points and seams at the center and at all other intersections. Press the seams open.

Sew one triangle (white, red, or green piece #6) to the bottom edge of every other tree to turn the octagon into a square. Press the seams toward piece #6. See Diagram 4.

Place the square of batting on the wrong side of the backing fabric. Then place the pieced potholder top right side up on top of the batting. Pin in place.

Stitch through all three layers, ⅛ inch from the outside edge. If you like, quilt the Christmas Tree design by hand or machine.

Pin a loop of ¼-inch red or green ribbon to one corner of the potholder.

Finish the edge with bias binding (page 24), using the 2-inch-wide bias strip to make a ½-inch binding.

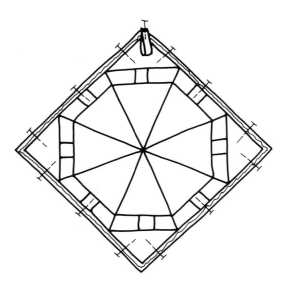

Diagram 4. Finish edges with bias binding

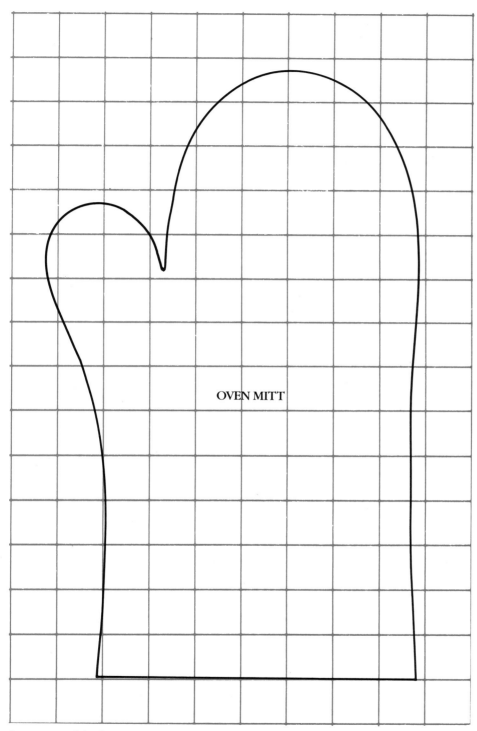

OVEN MITT

1 square = 1 inch

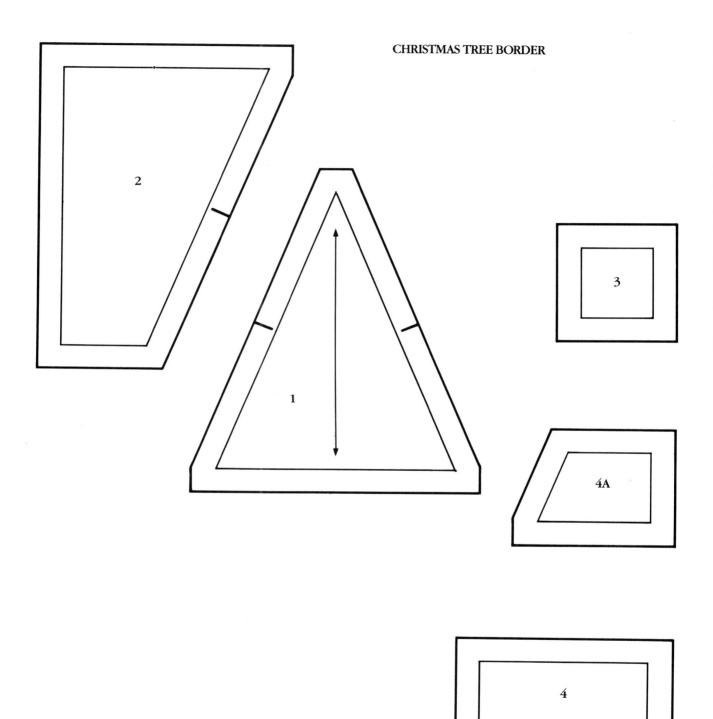

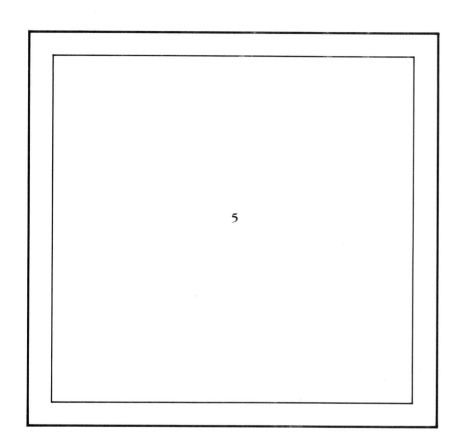

5

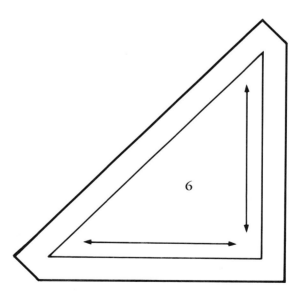

6

CHRISTMAS
TREE ORNAMENTS

The ornaments in this section can be hung from the tree as a group, or in multiples of one design. A tree would look beautiful, for example, decorated entirely with angels, each one made in different fabrics and trims.

They also have other wonderful uses. Fill them with aromatic mixtures and give them away as sachets. Tie them with ribbon to a gift box or a wreath. They make safe, colorful toys for children. However you choose to use them, they will add a touch of country charm to your holidays.

Calico Ball

Of all the ornaments in this chapter, the Calico Ball is probably the simplest one to make.

MATERIALS

Fabric

Pattern piece	Number of pieces
1	2 (in contrasting colors)

Diagram 1. Stitch two pieces together.

Other Materials

10¼ inches of ½-inch lace
10¼ inches of ¼-inch ribbon
Two 12-inch lengths of ¼-inch ribbon
3-inch-diameter Styrofoam ball
Tassel (optional)

SEWING INSTRUCTIONS

Pin and stitch the two #1 pieces along one long side. See Diagram 1. Press the seam open.

Topstitch a strip of lace down the center seam on the right side of the fabric. See Diagram 2.

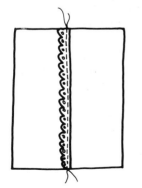

Diagram 2. Topstitch lace in place.

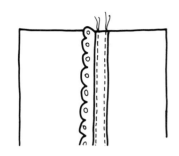

Diagram 3. Appliqué ribbon on top of seam line.

Pin the ribbon in place with one edge overlapping the unfinished edge of the lace. Topstitch or zigzag-stitch along both edges of the ribbon. See Diagram 3.

Fold over the top and bottom edges of the fabric (the long sides) ⅜ inch, with one 12-inch length of ¼-inch ribbon tucked inside each fold. The ends of the ribbon should stick out at both ends of the fabric hems. See Diagram 4.

Fold the fabric in half, right sides together, and sew the short ends of the fabric together to create a cylinder. Be careful to stitch up to, but not over, the ribbon casings. Press the seam open.

Turn the cylinder right side out and slip it over the Styrofoam ball. Pull both ends of each ribbon and tie them tightly. See Diagram 5. Tie the ends into a bow.

Attach a tassel (optional) to the bottom of the ornament. Suspend the ball from the tree with an ornament hanger hooked through the knot of the bow.

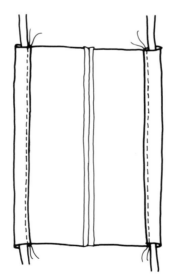

Diagram 4. Make casings for ribbon.

Diagram 5. Insert ball. Pull and tie ribbons.

Tree

This is another simple-to-make ornament.

MATERIALS

Fabric

Pattern piece	Number of pieces
1	1 (color optional)
2	1 (color optional)
3	4 (color optional)

Other Materials

⅓ yard of ½-inch lace

1½ inches of ¼-inch ribbon for loop

Polyester stuffing

SEWING INSTRUCTIONS

With right sides together and raw edges matching, pin and stitch the ½-inch-wide lace around the curved edge of piece #1. Then, pin a loop of ¼-inch ribbon to the point of piece #1. See Diagram 1.

Right sides together, fold piece #1 in half and stitch the side seam, catching the loop of ribbon at the top and leaving an opening to turn the tree right side out. See Diagram 2.

Pin the circle (piece #2) to the bottom edge of piece #1, matching the notches (the seam on piece #1 should match up with the fourth notch on piece #2). Place pins close together, adjusting the edges to fit. Stitch this seam just inside the first stitch line you made for the lace trim on piece #1. See Diagram 3. Clip the excess seam allowance from the tip and the curve.

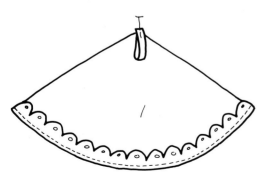

Diagram 1. Stitch lace to bottom and pin ribbon loop to top.

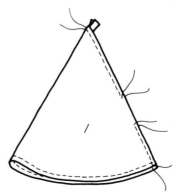

Diagram 2. Stitch seam, leaving opening.

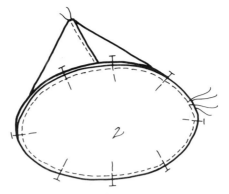

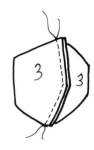

Diagram 3. Stitch bottom to tree.

Diagram 4. Stitch two #3 pieces together.

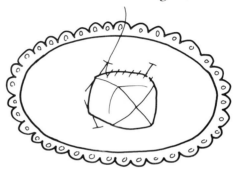

Diagram 5. Whipstitch trunk to bottom of tree.

Turn the tree right side out through the opening. Stuff with polyester stuffing, and whipstitch closed by hand.

To make the tree trunk, sew two #3 pieces together along one side, pivoting at the corner. Repeat for the other pair of #3's. See Diagram 4.

Sew the two pairs together (the points of the piece #3's will meet in the center of the bottom of the tree trunk. Turn the trunk right side out, turn the edges under ¼ inch and pin. Stuff the trunk as tightly as possible. Repin the trunk to the underside of the tree and sew it in place by hand. See Diagram 5.

Stars

Make dozens of stars in different fabrics to decorate your Christmas tree. Hang small stars from the branches and use a large star (made with the "A" pieces) as a treetop ornament. Experiment with different colors, prints, and stripes. For even more variety, try the Gored Star design.

MATERIALS

Fabric

Pattern piece	Number of pieces
1 (1A)	5 (Simple Star)
2 (2A)	10 (Gored Star)
3 (3A)	1 (each star)

Other Materials

1½ inches of ¼-inch satin ribbon for loop

Polyester stuffing

Polyester batting for the Treetop Star

1 yard of ½-inch lace (optional) for the Treetop Star

SEWING INSTRUCTIONS

Simple Star

Sew two diamonds (piece #1) together along one side, stopping ¼ inch from one end of the seam (this will be the center of the star). See Diagram 1. Repeat for a second pair of diamonds. Press the seams open.

Sew the remaining diamond (piece #1) to one side of one of the pairs, stopping ¼ inch from the same end (center). Press the seam open. See Diagram 2.

With right sides together, sew the two sections of diamonds together, pivoting on the point of the diamond at the center of the star. See Diagram 3.

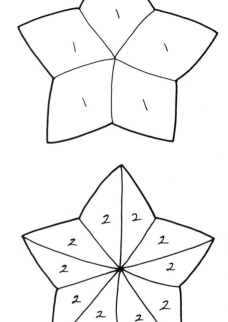

Piecing diagrams.

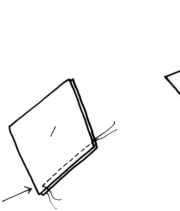

Diagram 1. Sew two diamonds together along one side.

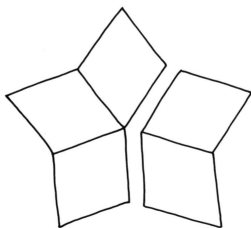

Diagram 2. Sew remaining diamond to one pair.

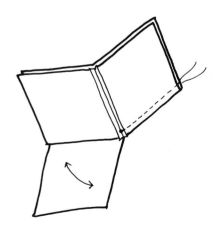

Diagram 3. Sew two sections of stars together.

59

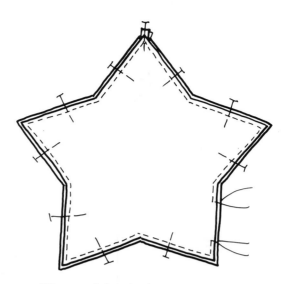

Diagram 4. Sew backing to pieced star.

To turn the corner, leave the needle down and lift the presser foot. Pivot and adjust the fabric so free edge of diamond on top lines up with free edge of diamond on bottom. Release the presser foot and continue sewing. Press the seams open.

Pin a 1½-inch loop to the tip of one of the points. With right sides facing, pin and stitch piece #3 to the pieced star. Sew all around the outside edge of the star, leaving an opening on one side of the points for turning. See Diagram 4.

Clip the excess seam allowance from the tips and clip the seams at the corners. Be careful to clip up to, but not through, the stitch line.

Turn the star right side out through the opening. Stuff the star with polyester stuffing and whipstitch the opening closed by hand.

Gored Star

Using contrasting fabrics, sew two triangles (piece #2) together along the longest side. Repeat to make five diamond-shaped points. Press the seams open.

To finish, proceed as for the Simple Star.

Treetop Star

Both the Simple Star and the Gored Star make spectacular treetop ornaments. Make them with the larger ("A") pattern pieces.

Cut and assemble the pieces as for the smaller stars.

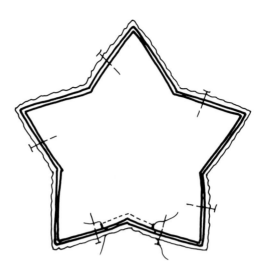

Diagram 5. Stitch between two notches.

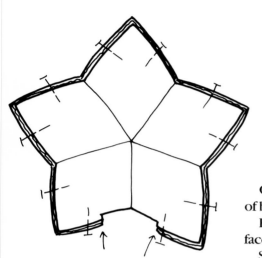

Diagram 6. Turn lining to back.

Cut two linings (any light-colored cotton or cotton blend) and two layers of batting using the large pattern (piece #3A).

Place the pieced star right side up on top of the batting. Place the lining facedown on top of the star front and pin in place.

Sew the three layers together between the two notches. Clip the corner between the points. Clip up to, but not through, the stitch line. See Diagram 5. Repeat for the back of the star, without the batting.

Turn the lining of the star front to the back with the wrong side toward the batting and the right side of the star front facing up. Turn the lining of the star back to the back with wrong sides facing. On both the star front and the star back the seams between the notches will be finished, the rest of the seams will have raw edges. Press the seams on both the star front and the star back.

Repin through all three layers on the star front. Stitch ⅛ inch from the edge around the unfinished sides to the notches. Repeat for both layers of the star back. See Diagram 6.

Lace can be added to the edge of the star front at this point, if you like. With right sides together and raw edges matching, pin and stitch the ½-inch-wide lace around all of the sides except at the finished seam between the notches. Make small pleats at the points so that there will be enough lace to turn the corners at the points of the star after the star is turned right side out.

Pin the front and the back of the star together with right sides facing and stitch ¼ inch from the edge around all the sides up to the notches. If the star has a lace edge, be careful not to catch the lace pleats in the seams near the points.

Clip the corners, trim the seams, and turn the star right side out. Slip the star onto the top of the Christmas tree through the opening. See Diagram 7.

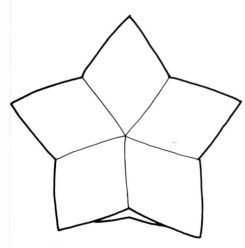

Diagram 7. Turn right side out.

Hearts

Hearts are appropriate for every occasion. At Christmastime they delight us in bright reds and greens, plain or trimmed with ribbons and lace. Make hearts for the tree, and hearts to tie on gifts, hearts to decorate a wreath, ornament a table setting, or to fill with aromatic mixtures for sweet sachets. Here are patchwork hearts for you to stitch in plaids and calicos, stripes and polka dots — good, strong hearts "stuffed" with Christmas cheer.

No two hearts need be the same. The choice of prints and the addition of different ribbons and trims can make each one unique and wonderful. Yet each of the hearts pictured on page 64 is made from one of these three basic patterns.

Piecing diagrams.

MATERIALS

Fabric

Pattern piece	Number of pieces
1	1 (Whole Heart)
2	2 (Half a Heart)
3	1 (Cupid's Arrow)
4	1 (Cupid's Arrow)

For hearts, cut a backing piece from pattern #1.

Other Materials

Small amounts of ¼-inch ribbon for loops
Trims: lace, ribbons, braid, etc.
Polyester stuffing

SEWING INSTRUCTIONS

Whole Heart

Cut out a front and back heart from matching or contrasting fabric, using pattern piece #1.

Diagram 1. Pin ribbon loop to heart front.

Diagram 2. Stitch front and back together.

Diagram 3. Hearts with appliquéd lace and ribbon trim.

Make a 1½-inch loop of ¼-inch ribbon and pin it to the center-top of the heart front. See Diagram 1.

With right sides together, stitch the heart front and back together, leaving an opening on one side to turn the heart right side out. See Diagram 2.

Ribbon and Trim: Before sewing the heart front to the heart back, pin and stitch the ribbon or trim to the front of the heart. If you are using lace and ribbon together, sew the lace down first and then add the ribbon to conceal the unfinished edge of the lace. Notice the great variety of effects that can be achieved by changing the position and style of the trim. See Diagram 3.

Ruffled Lace Edging: Before you sew the heart front to the heart back, pin and sew the lace, ruffled edge in, around the outside edge of the heart front. At the point, make a pleat so that the lace will turn the corner neatly when the heart is turned right side out. Trim the lace at the center where it meets the other end. See Diagram 4.

Pin a ribbon loop to the center-top of the heart. Pin the heart back to the heart front, right sides facing. Pin very carefully at the point to make sure that the lace pleat doesn't get caught in the seam on either side. Stitch the front and back together, leaving an opening on one side for turning.

Clip up to, but not through, the seam at the center of the heart. Trim the corner at the point. Turn the heart right side out. Stuff lightly with polyester stuffing, and whipstitch the opening closed by hand.

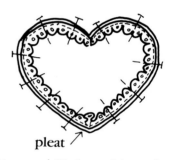

pleat

Diagram 4. Pin lace edging to heart front.

65

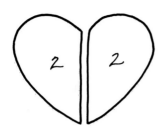

Diagram 5. Sew two halves together to make whole heart.

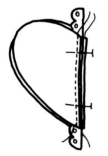

Diagram 6. Appliqué lace and trim over center seam.

Half a Heart

Cut two of piece #2 in contrasting colors and stitch them together to make a whole heart. See Diagram 5. Finish as for Whole Heart.

You can add trim to this pieced heart in several different ways. You can appliqué ribbon and lace combined, or a strip of double-sided lace, right on top of the center seam. See Diagram 6.

Or you may prefer to sew the trim (such as lace, piping, or ruffles) into the seam in the following manner. Before you sew the two halves of the heart front together, pin the trim along one edge of one half of the heart front. Stitch the two halves of the heart together, and clip the lace at the top and bottom of the heart. See Diagram 7.

To complete the heart, cut a back using pattern piece #1, and assemble as for Whole Heart.

Cupid's Arrow

Cut and sew the two halves of this design together as for Half a Heart, substituting pattern pieces #3 and #4 for pattern piece #2. See Diagram 8.

Diagram 7. Stitch trim to center seam.

Hearts with trim stitched into center seam.

Diagram 8. Cupid's Arrow Hearts.

66

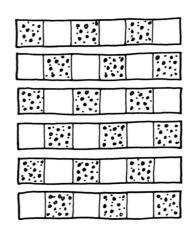

Diagram 10. Assembling
checkerboard patchwork.

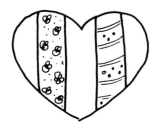

Diagram 9. Striped patchwork hearts.

Patchwork Hearts

Stripes

Sew six 1½ × 5½-inch strips of different-colored fabrics together. Press the seams open.

Position pattern piece #1 vertically or diagonally on the pieced stripes and cut. See Diagram 9. Assemble as for Whole Heart.

Checkerboard

Sew six 1½ × 8-inch fabric strips together as above. Press the seams open.

Cut the stripes horizontally into 1½-inch strips. Turn every other strip so that the colors alternate. See Diagram 10. Sew the strips together to make a checkerboard pattern, matching the seams at the intersections. Press the seams open.

Position pattern piece #1 either vertically or diagonally on top of the pieced checkerboard fabric, and cut out the heart shape. Assemble as for Whole Heart.

Angels

The little Angel Ornament with eyelet lace wings will be very happy suspended from the branches of your Christmas tree. Use a wooden drawer pull for her head, and a bow for her hands. The larger Treetop Angel is a perfect finishing touch for your Christmas tree.

MATERIALS

Fabric

ANGEL ORNAMENT

Pattern piece	Number of pieces
1	2 (plus 2 in contrasting color for lining)
2	1
3	2
4	1 (lining)
5	2

TREETOP ANGEL

Pattern piece	Number of pieces
1A	2 (plus 2 in contrasting color for lining)
2A	1
3A	2
4A	1 (lining, plus 1 from batting)
5A	2

Other Materials

FOR ANGEL ORNAMENT

⅓ yard of 2-inch white eyelet lace for wings

8 inches of ¼-inch beige ribbon for hands

Small wooden drawer pull (with screw) for head

FOR TREETOP ANGEL

½ yard of 4-inch white eyelet lace for wings

8 inches of ½-inch beige ribbon for hands

Large drawer pull for head

Lightweight batting

Thin florist's wire (optional)

FOR BOTH

Yellow, brown, red, or black baby yarn or pearl cotton for hair

Small amount of ¼-inch ribbon (any color) for hair

⅓ yard of ½-inch lace trim

½-inch washer with hole smaller than the screw head

Fabric glue (Sobo)

Metal hanger for making hair

SEWING INSTRUCTIONS

Angel Ornament

Cut two of pattern piece #1 from dress fabric and two from lining fabric.

With right sides facing, pin one lining to one sleeve and sew along outside edge. See Diagram 1. Clip the corners, turn and press. Repeat for the other sleeve.

Fold each sleeve in half with the lining side out. Sew along the curved edge. See Diagram 2. Trim the seam allowance, turn and press.

Insert about 4 inches of ¼-inch beige ribbon into each sleeve, catching one end in the upper corner with a pin. See Diagram 3.

Cut one dress front (pattern piece #2) from dress fabric. Place a sleeve between the notches on piece #2 and pin in place. Repeat for the second sleeve. See Diagram 4.

To make the angel's wings: Cut two of pattern piece #5 from eyelet lace. Turn under the raw edges and hem. Press. Pin the wings in place over the sleeves (the lace will extend about ½ inch beyond the top and bottom edges of the sleeve). Stitch the sleeves and wings in place with a ⅛-inch seam.

Cut two backs (pattern piece #3) from dress fabric and pin one to either side of the dress front (pattern piece #2). Stitch in place.

Diagram 1. Pin lining to sleeve and stitch.

Diagram 2. Fold sleeve in half and stitch along curved edge.

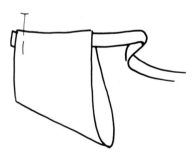

Diagram 3. Insert ribbon in sleeve.

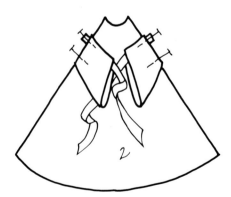

Diagram 4. Pin sleeves to dress front.

Diagram 5. Stitch back to front; add lace to hem.

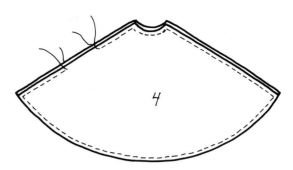

Diagram 6. Line angel ornament.

Press the sleeves toward the front and the wings toward the back. Pin and sew a row of ½-inch lace around the curved hem of the dress. See Diagram 5.

Cut one pattern piece #4 from lining fabric. Pin the lining in place over pieces #2 and #3, right sides facing. Sew all around, leaving an opening on one side of the center-back for turning. See Diagram 6.

Clip the corners and trim the excess seam allowance. Turn the angel right side out and press. Close the center-back seam by hand.

To assemble the angel's head: Place the washer over the drawer pull screw. Insert the screw through the neck of the dress from the inside and screw it tightly into the drawer pull.

To make the angel's hair: Bend a metal coat hanger into a rectangle approximately 10 inches wide. Wrap yarn around the rectangle about fifteen times, keeping the strands close together.

Slide the hanger under the presser foot of your sewing machine and stitch down the center of the yarn loops. Cut the yarn off the hanger at the sides. See Diagram 7.

Glue the hair along the part to the top of the drawer pull and allow it to dry. Trim the ends and braid or tie with ribbon. Make a small thread loop at the top of the angel's head (at the part) to hang her from the Christmas tree.

Tie the ribbons at the sleeves into a small bow to form the hands. If you like, you can paint facial features on the front of the drawer pull.

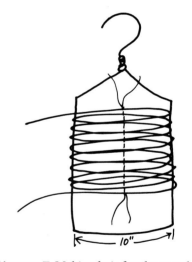

Diagram 7. Making hair for the angel.

Treetop Angel

The larger Treetop Angel is made the same way as the Angel Ornament, with only one change: batting is used in the dress of the Treetop Angel to give it extra support.

71

Construct the Treetop Angel as for the Angel Ornament through Diagram 5, using the larger "A" pattern pieces. Then, cut a piece of quilt batting from pattern piece #4A (lining). Place the completed dress (as shown in Diagram 5) on top of the batting, and pin it in place. Stitch a ⅛-inch seam around all sides.

Continue to assemble the Treetop Angel following the instructions for the Angel Ornament from Diagram 5 on.

To make longer hair for the Treetop Angel, bend the hanger into a rectangle about 15 inches wide.

Finish the Treetop Angel as for the Angel Ornament.

Insert the thin wire (optional) in the hem at the top of each wing to add stiffness.

Country House

This cozy little house sits very comfortably on its own branch or nestles beneath the tree.

MATERIALS

Fabric

Pattern piece	Number of pieces
1	1 (door)
2	4 (house)
3	2 (house)
4	5 (windows)
5	1 (house)
6	6 (house)
7	4 (house)
8	2 (roof)
9	1 (house)

Other Materials

½ yard of narrow lace (optional) for the bottom edge of the roof, and to use in the windows as curtains

Polyester stuffing

SEWING INSTRUCTIONS

Cut out all pattern pieces from appropriate fabrics and set them aside. All of the house pieces (#2, #3, #5, #6, #7, #9) should be cut from the same fabric. The door, windows and roof should be cut from contrasting fabrics.

Sew a piece #2 to each side of piece #1 (door). Press the seams open. Sew a piece #3 on top and press the seam open. See Diagram 1.

To make the curtains in the windows (optional), sew lace down both sides of each piece #4. Sew one piece #6 to the left side of four of piece #4. Press the seams open. See Diagram 2.

Sew two of these sections together so that the pieces alternate: 6-4-6-4. Repeat for the other two sections. Now sew one piece #6 to the right end of each of the two assembled sections. See Diagram 3. Press the seams open.

Sew one piece #7 to the top and another to the bottom of each of the two sections assembled above to complete the sides of the house. See Diagram 4. Press the seams open.

Sew the last piece #4 to piece #5. Press the seam open. Sew a piece #2 to each side of the 4-5 pair. Press the seams open. Sew a piece #3 to the top, and press the seam open. See Diagram 5.

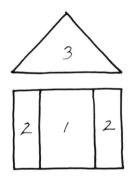

Diagram 1. Assemble front of house.

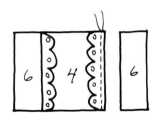

Diagram 2. Stitch one #6 to left side of #4.

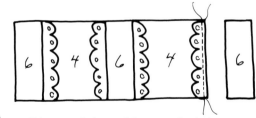

Diagram 3. Assemble row of windows.

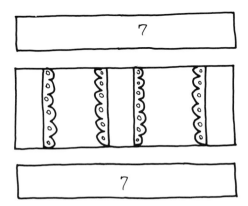

Diagram 4. Assemble side of house.

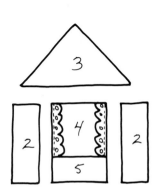

Diagram 5. Assemble back of house.

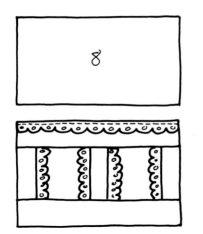

Diagram 6. Sew roof to side of house.

Sew a strip of lace (optional) to one long side of each side of the house. Sew a piece #8 to the top of one side of the house. See Diagram 6. Repeat for the other side. Press the seams open.

Starting at the peak, sew one end section of the house to one side section. To turn the corner where the roof joins the side, leave the needle down at the seam line, and lift the presser foot. Clip the seam up to the needle. Pivot and adjust the fabric. Lower the presser foot and continue to sew, stopping ¼ inch from the end of the seam. Repeat for the other end and side sections. See Diagram 7.

Starting and stopping ¼ inch from the ends of the seams, sew the two halves of the house together, turning the corner where the roof joins the house. Repeat for the other side. See Diagram 8. Pin and sew the seam at the top of the roof where both #8 pieces meet.

With right sides facing, sew piece #9 to the underside of the house. Stitch the two short ends first and the sides second, leaving an opening in one of the sides so the house can be turned right side out. See Diagram 9.

To eliminate bulk, clip the corners. Be careful to clip up to, but not through, the stitch lines. Turn the house right side out through the opening. Stuff the house, and close the opening by hand.

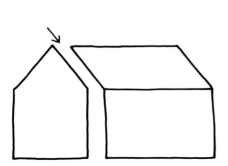

Diagram 7. Join end of house to side and roof sections.

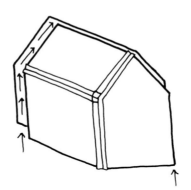

Diagram 8. Sew two halves of house together.

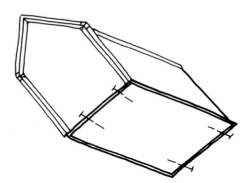

Diagram 9. Sew bottom (#9) to underside of house, leaving opening to turn.

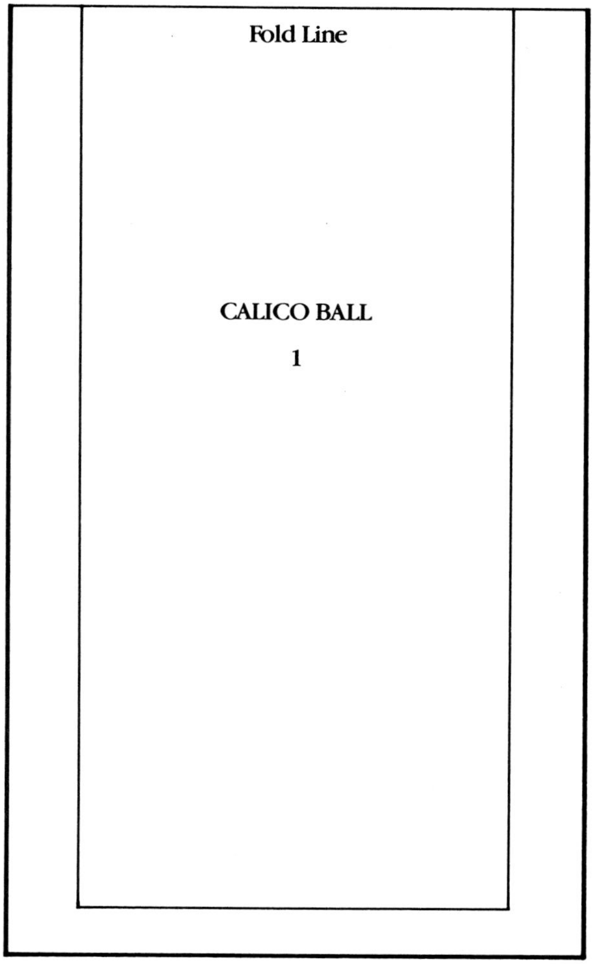

Fold Line

CALICO BALL

1

TREE

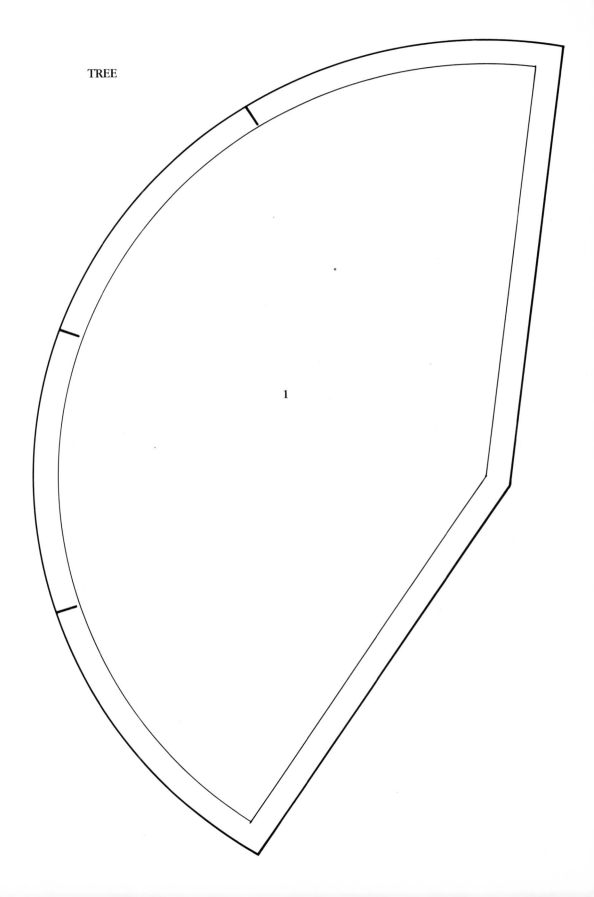

1

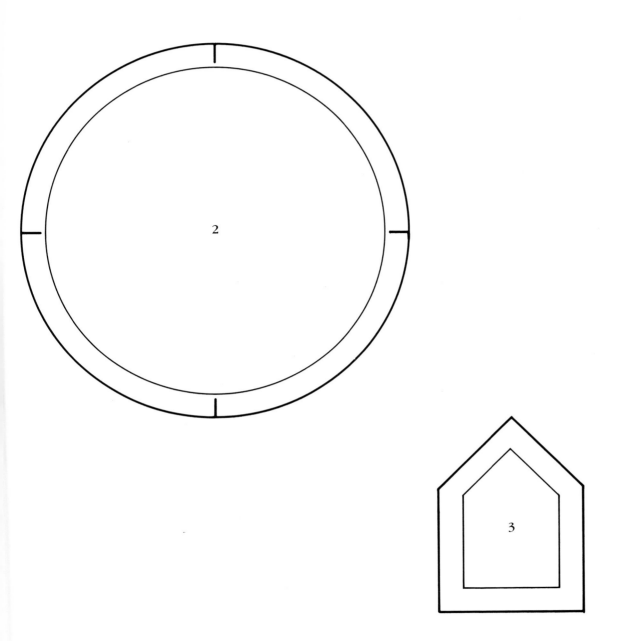

2

3

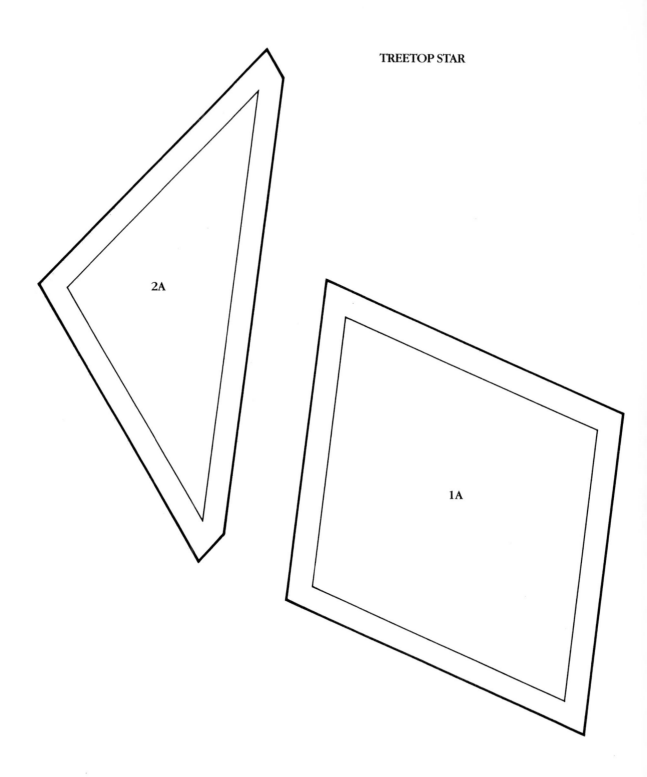

2A

1A

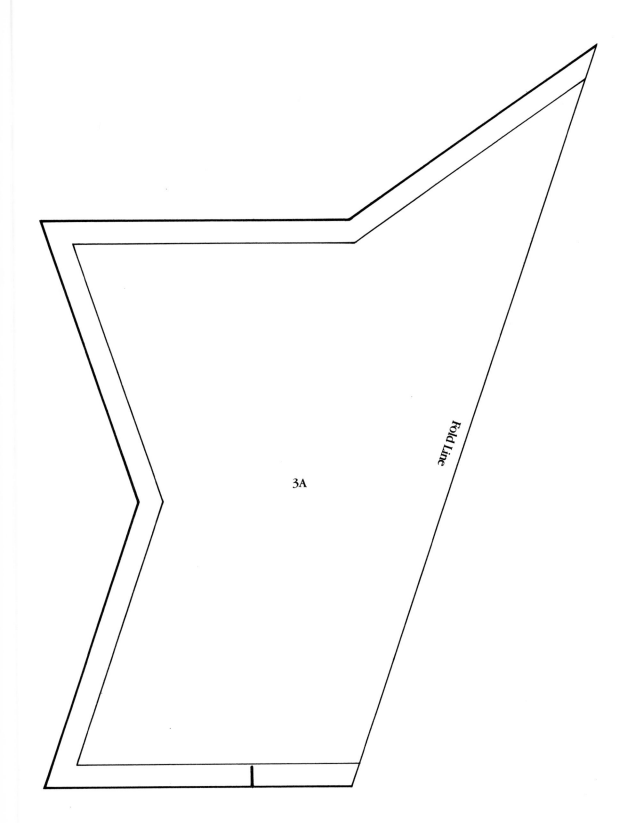

3A

Fold Line

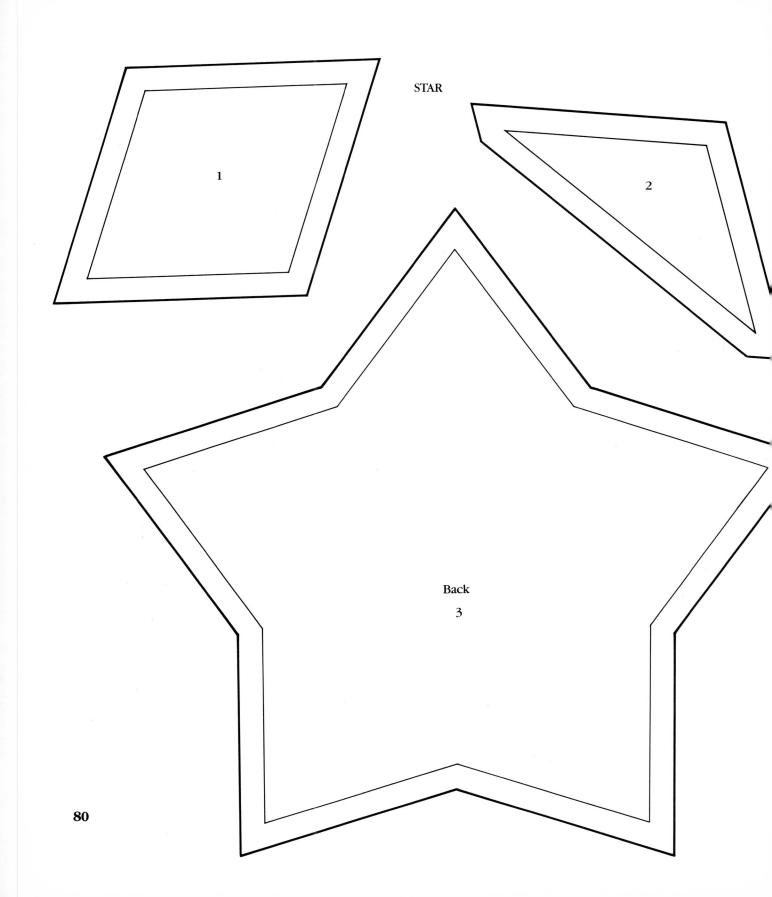

STAR

1

2

Back

3

80

HEARTS

1

2

CUPID'S ARROW

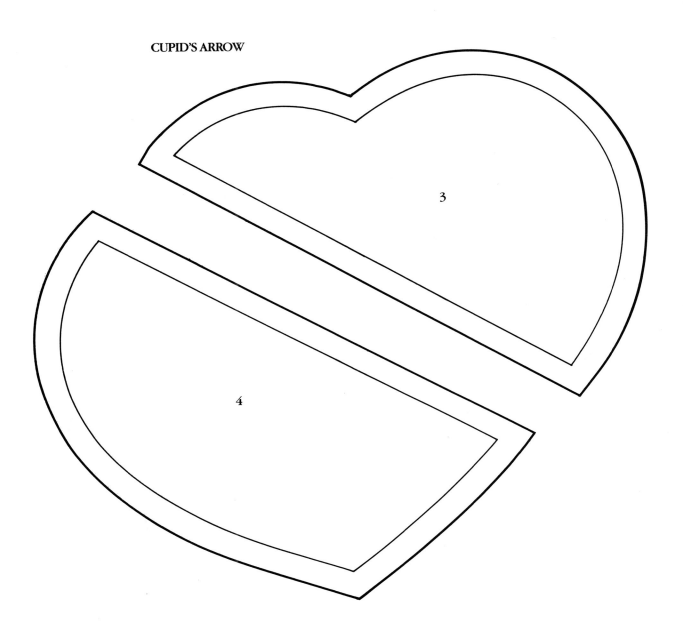

3

4

82

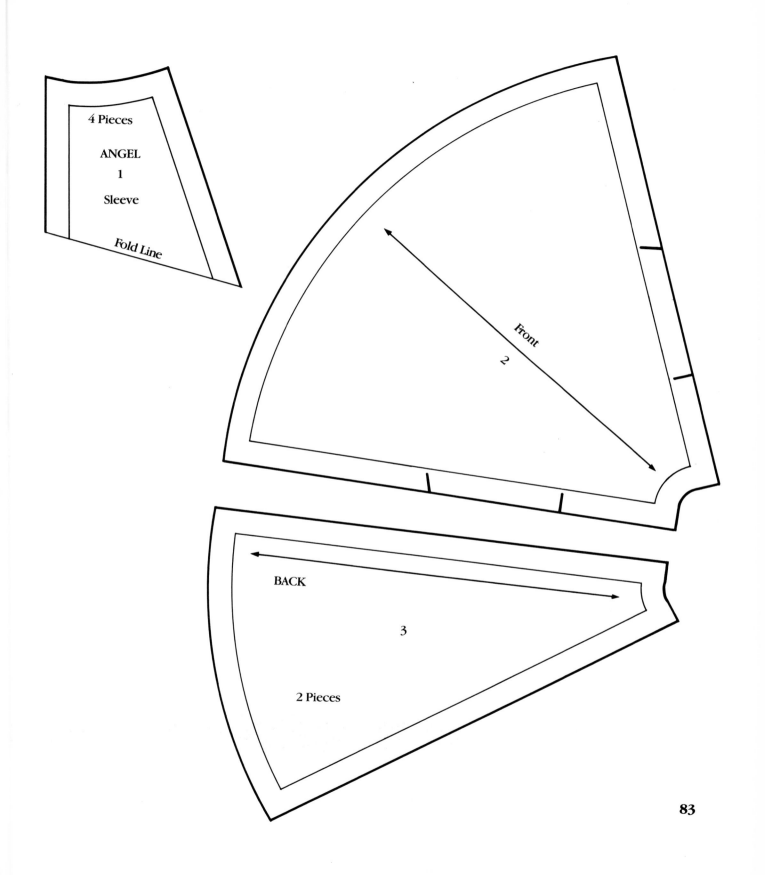

4 Pieces

ANGEL

1

Sleeve

Fold Line

Front

2

BACK

3

2 Pieces

83

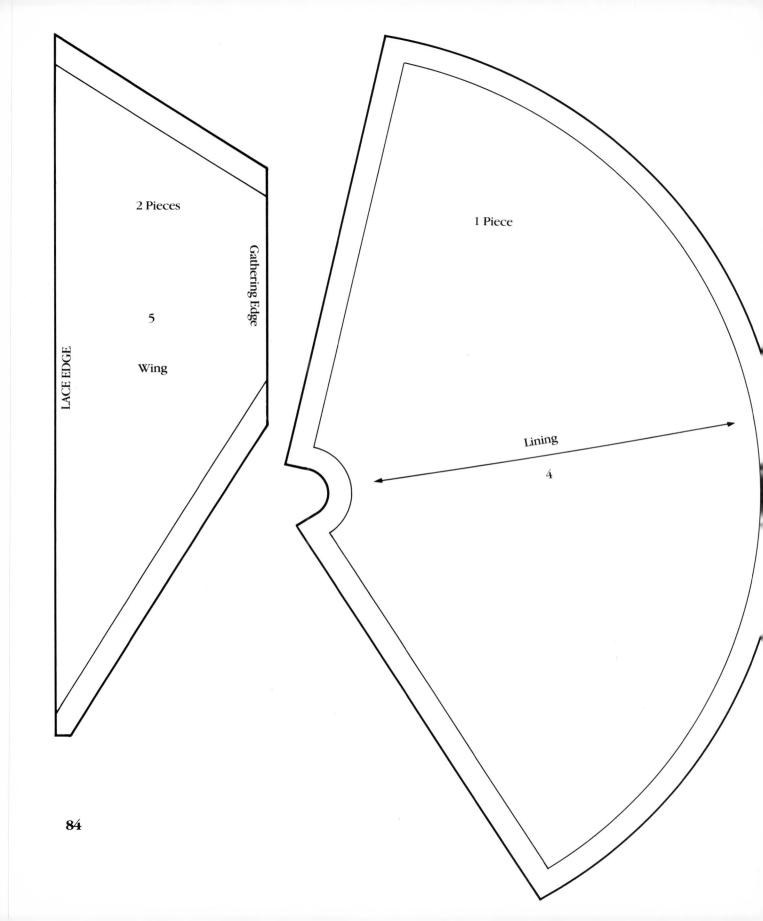

2 Pieces

5

Wing

Gathering Edge

LACE EDGE

1 Piece

Lining

4

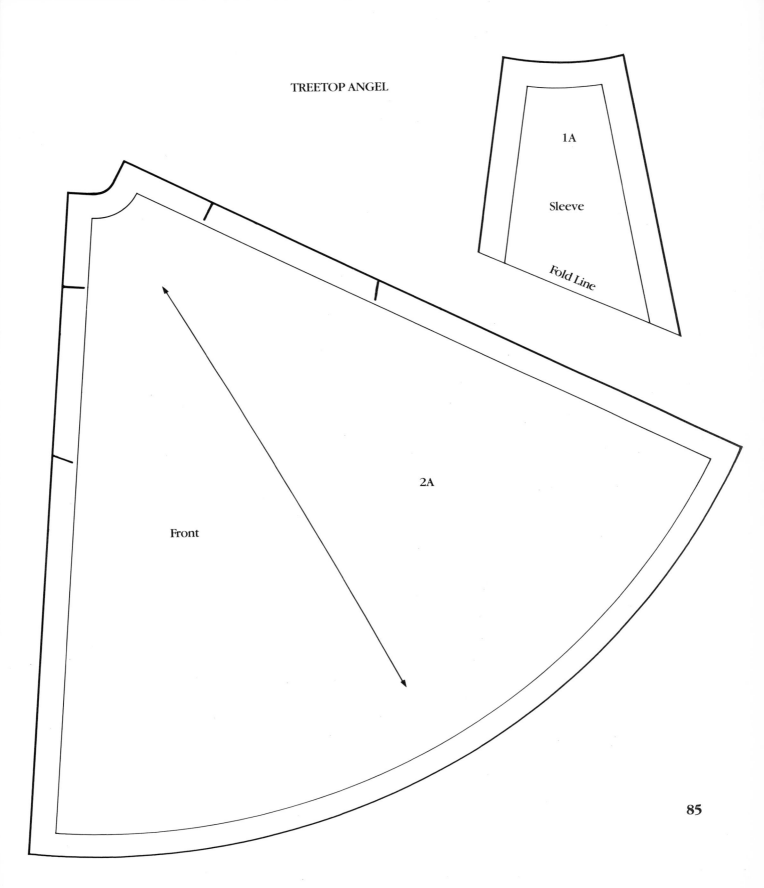

TREETOP ANGEL

1A

Sleeve

Fold Line

2A

Front

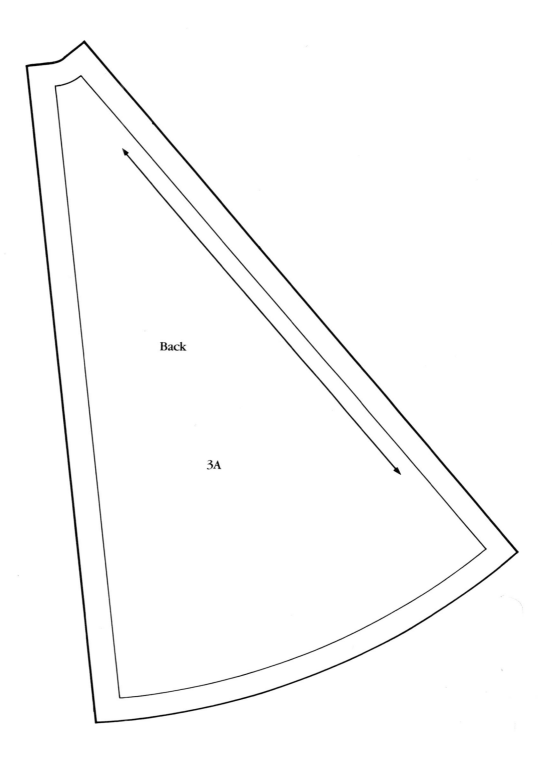

Back

3A

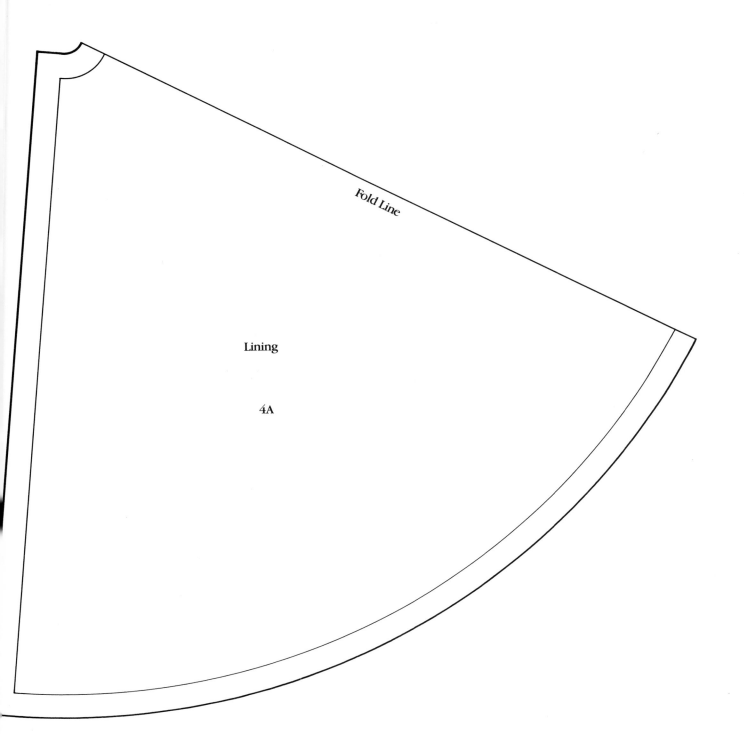

Fold Line

Lining

4A

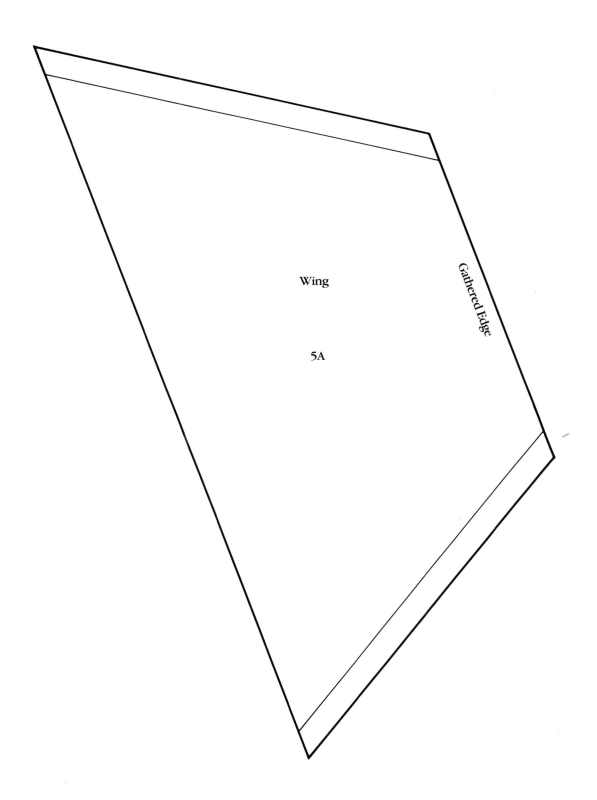

Wing

5A

Gathered Edge

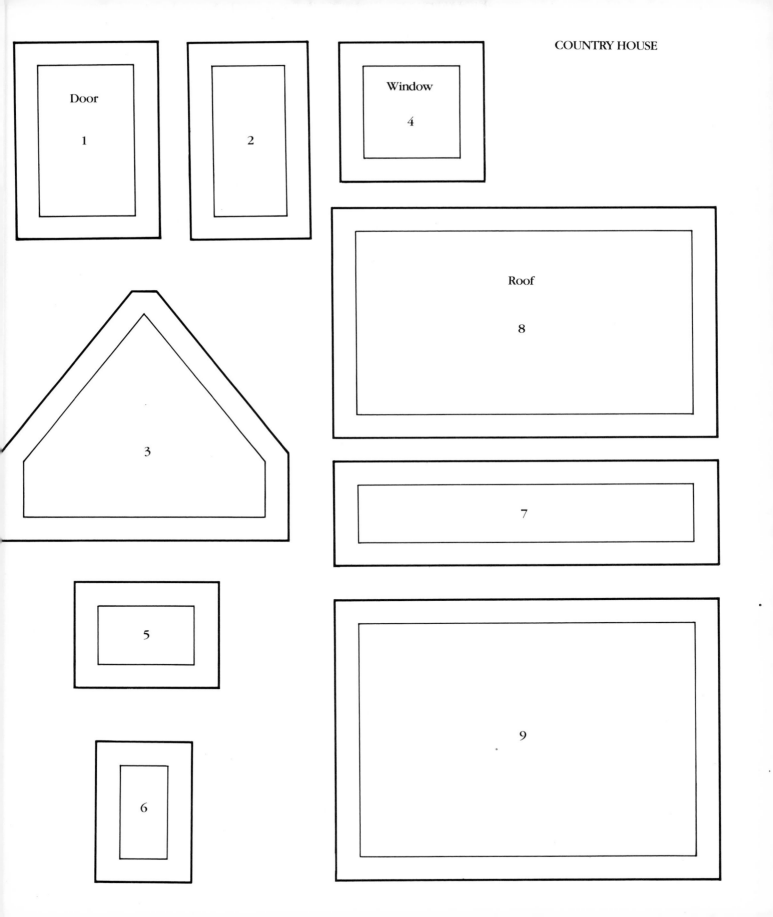

COUNTRY HOUSE

Door

1

2

Window

4

Roof

8

3

7

5

9

6

CHRISTMAS STOCKINGS

A variety of Christmas stockings can be made using the basic stocking pattern and then decorating the fabric stocking with other designs, such as the Christmas Tree Border, Holiday Hearts and Christmas Pine patterns.

The basic stocking can be made from pre-quilted fabric, from fabric you've quilted yourself, or from two layers of fabric with batting sandwiched between them.

The Christmas Stocking pattern (page 97) is shown reduced. To enlarge the pattern, draw a grid of 1-inch squares (or use purchased graph paper). Copy the pattern onto the grid and cut the pattern from paper or lightweight cardboard.

Stocking with Christmas Tree Border

Border with Three Trees (see page 50 for patterns)

MATERIALS

Fabric

Pattern piece	Number of pieces
1	2 red, 4 green, 4 white
2	4 (cut two, flop pattern, cut another two)
3	2 red, 4 green
4	8 white

½ yard of pre-quilted fabric

Other Materials

20 inches of 1-inch-wide eyelet lace

Small amount of ¼-inch-wide satin ribbon

SEWING INSTRUCTIONS

To begin, make two strips of Christmas Tree Borders (page 40) with three trees in each strip. See Diagram 1.

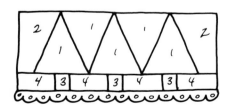

Diagram 1. Make Christmas Tree Border three trees wide.

92

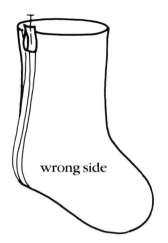

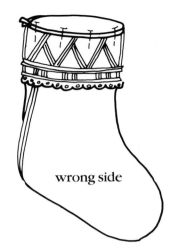

Diagram 2. Pin ribbon loop to back seam.

Diagram 3. Pin border to top of stocking.

Next, cut one stocking front and one stocking back from pre-quilted fabric. Right sides facing, sew the front and back together. Trim the seam. Pin a loop of ¼-inch ribbon to the top of the back seam. See Diagram 2.

Sew the two Christmas Tree Borders together end to end. Press the seams open. Pin the border to the top of the stocking (right side of border to wrong side of stocking). Stitch a ¼-inch seam around the edge. See Diagram 3.

Turn the stocking right side out. Fold the border to the right side and stitch the bottom edge of the border, just below the tree trunks, to the stocking.

Checkerboard Heart Stocking

MATERIALS

Fabric
1½ yards of white fabric to make quilted fabric,
    border and lining
½ yard of red fabric for heart and border

Other Materials
Batting
Small amount of ¼-inch-wide satin ribbon

SEWING INSTRUCTIONS

To create your own quilted fabric for the Checkerboard Heart Stocking: Cut four pieces of white fabric and two pieces of quilt batting in 15 × 22-inch rectangles (large enough to accommodate the stocking pattern). Place one piece of batting between two layers of fabric for each side of the stocking. Mark the top layers of fabric with a diagonal grid of 1½-inch squares. Pin all

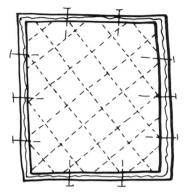

Diagram 1. Prepare fabric for quilting.

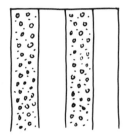

Diagram 2. Stitch strips of red and white fabric together.

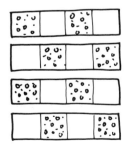

Diagram 3. Arrange cut strips to form checkerboard pattern.

three layers together and stitch the grid pattern by hand or machine. See Diagram 1.

Use the stocking pattern to trace and cut one front and one back from the quilted fabric.

Cut out one heart from the heart pattern (page 98) or use the Star Ornament pattern (page 80). Pin the shape in place on one side of the stocking, turn the edges under, and whipstitch around the edge of the shape.

With right sides facing, sew the front and back of the stocking together around the outside edge, leaving the top open. Clip and trim the seams, and then turn the stocking right side out.

To make the Checkerboard Border: Sew two red and two white strips, 1½ × 27 inches each, together along the long sides. Alternate red and white strips. Press the seams open. See Diagram 2.

Cut the strips crosswise into eighteen 1½-inch-wide strips. Flop every other strip and arrange them so that the colors alternate, forming a checkerboard pattern. See Diagram 3.

Pin and stitch two strips together, matching the seams at the intersections. Repeat for nine sets of strips. Press the seams open.

Sew the nine sets of checks together to make a band of eighteen rows of four squares each. Press the seams open. Then sew the ends of the band together and press the seam open.

Cut a strip of white fabric, 4½ × 18½ inches, for the lining of the checkerboard band. Stitch the ends of the lining together. Press the seam open. With right sides facing, pin and sew the lining to the band along one side. See Diagram 4.

Turn the border right side out and press. Pin a loop of ¼-inch-wide ribbon to the top of the back seam inside the stocking. Place the band inside the top of the stocking with the right side of the checkerboard facing the wrong side of the stocking. Pin in place. Sew the band around the top of the stocking. Fold the band back over to the right side of the stocking.

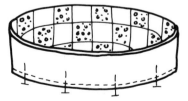

Diagram 4. Sew lining to border.

Diagram 1. Assemble fabric for stocking front.

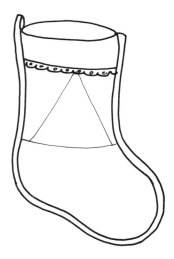

Diagram 2. Finish stocking edges with bias binding.

Christmas Pine Stocking

One Pine Tree (see page 164 for patterns)

MATERIALS

Fabric

Pattern piece	Number of pieces
1	1 green
2	1 green
3	2 white
5	8 green,
	10 white
6	2 white
7	1 green

¾ yard white fabric for lining
¾ yard fabric for background
¾ yard fabric in a contrasting color

Other Materials
9½ inches of ¾-inch-wide lace
2 yards of 2-inch-wide bias trim

SEWING INSTRUCTIONS

To make one Christmas Pine motif, follow the instructions for the Christmas Pine Quilt (page 164).

Cut two pieces of background fabric from pattern piece #1A (page 99) — one right and one left. Cut one rectangle, 3⅓ × 9½ inches, in a contrasting color. Cut one rectangle, 10 × 15 inches, in background color. Cut the stocking back from a 15 × 22-inch rectangle of background color. Cut two stocking shapes from white lining fabric, and two from quilt batting.

Sew one piece #1A (page 99) to each side of the Christmas Pine tree. Press the seams to one side, away from the tree.

Stitch the lace (optional) to one long side of the 3½ × 9½-inch rectangle. Sew the lace-edged rectangle to the top, and the 10 × 15-inch rectangle to the bottom of the Christmas Pine tree. See Diagram 1. Press the seams open.

Use the enlarged stocking pattern to cut out a stocking front from the pieced fabric.

With right sides facing, place the lining on top of the stocking front and place the batting underneath. Pin all three layers together and stitch along the top, ¼ inch from the top edge. Remove the pins, fold the lining over to the back, and repin all three layers together.

Sew the three layers together around the sides ⅛ inch from the edge. Do not stitch across the top. Repeat for the stocking back.

With wrong sides facing, pin the front of the stocking to the back and stitch around three sides ¼ inch from the edge. Leave the top open.

Finish the edges with a strip of 2-inch-wide bias trim. See Binding the Quilt, page 24. Make a loop at the top of the seam at the back of the stocking with the end of the bias binding. See Diagram 2.

Note: To accommodate the size of one Christmas Pine tree motif you will need to enlarge the width of the stocking pattern by about ½ inch on *each* side.

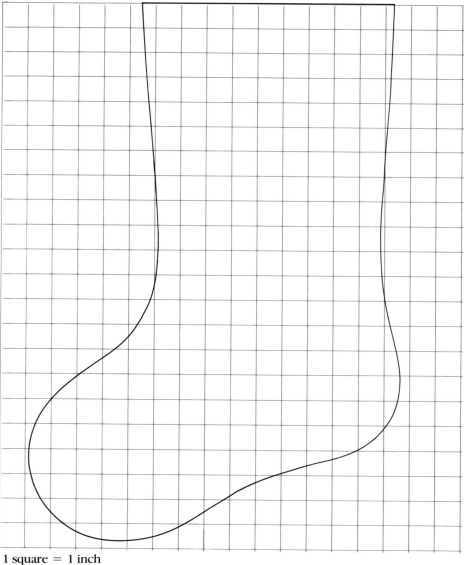

1 square = 1 inch

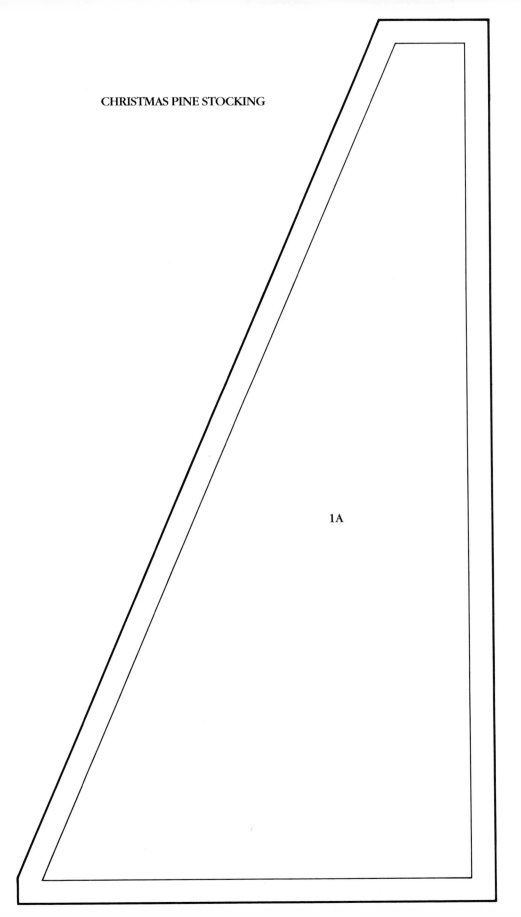

CHRISTMAS PINE STOCKING

1A

HOLIDAY HEARTS

Wall Hanging

Hearts and checkerboards combine in an easy-to-make wall hanging. The companion pillow and potholder on the following pages brighten up the house at holiday time.

MATERIALS

Fabric

Hearts: 4 green, 4 red, 1 white (#1)

6¾-inch squares: 4 red, 4 white, 1 green (#2)

7⅓ yards each of 1½-inch-wide red and white fabric strips for the checkerboard border (pattern piece #3)

2 white borders (7 × 23½ inches)

2 white borders (7 × 36½ inches)

37-inch square of white fabric for backing

Other Materials

4⅛ yards of red 1½-inch bias trim for binding the outer edge

37-inch square of quilt batting

Freezer paper

Glue stick

SEWING INSTRUCTIONS

Using the heart pattern (#1) which has no seam allowance, cut nine hearts from freezer paper. Place each one, shiny side down, on the wrong side of the fabric: four on red, four on green, and one on white. Press (the freezer paper will stick to the fabric).

Cut around the hearts, trimming the fabric to within ³⁄₁₆ inch from the edges. Clip the seam allowance at close intervals up to, but not through, the edge of the paper hearts. See Diagram 1.

Diagram 1. Clip seam allowance up to edge of paper.

Lightly apply glue with the glue stick to the wrong side of the seam allowance. Fold the seam allowance over the paper heart and press in place to create a smooth curve around the heart.

Center the hearts on the squares (#2) as follows: green hearts on red squares, red hearts on white squares, and the white heart on the green square. Pin and whipstitch the hearts to the squares. See Diagram 2.

Cut a slit in the center-back of each square, clipping through the background fabric only. Soak the squares in warm water for a few minutes to loosen the freezer paper. Pull the freezer paper through the opening and discard it. Allow the squares to dry, then press the hearts carefully.

Trim the fabric away from the back of the square and clip the excess seam allowance from the heart to within ¼ inch of the stitching line. See Diagram 3.

Pin and stitch the squares together in three rows to make a checkerboard pattern with a red square (green heart) at each corner and the green square (white heart) in the center. See Diagram 4.

To make the checkerboard border: Stitch 1½-inch-wide strips (#3) of red and white fabric together in four rows, alternating red and white. See Diagram 5. Press the seams open.

Cut the pieced strips into 1½-inch-wide sections. Sew the sections together in sets of two, matching the seams at the intersections and reversing the position of the red and white squares. See Diagram 6.

Sew the sets together end to end, matching the seams at the intersections to make checkerboard borders as follows: two rows of 5 sets, or 20 squares

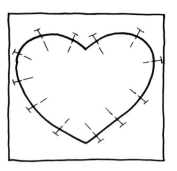

Diagram 2. Pin and stitch hearts to squares.

Diagram 3. Clip away backing and excess seam allowance.

Diagram 4. Arrange squares with hearts in checkerboard pattern.

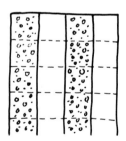

Diagram 5. Piece red and white fabric strips together.

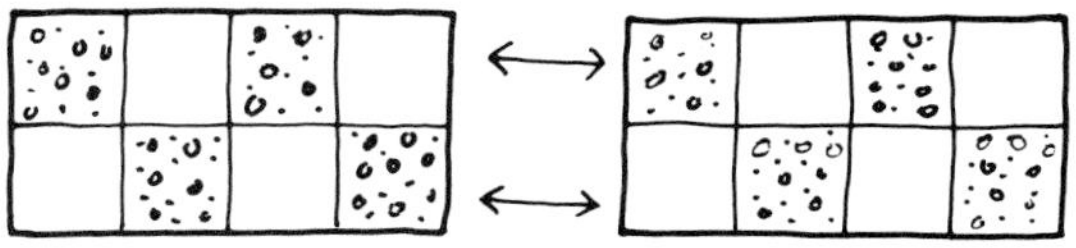

Diagram 6. Clip strips into squares and reassemble to make checkerboard borders.

(20 inches long), and two rows of 6 sets, or 24 squares (24 inches long). Eliminate the last square from the end of each row since two rows actually require a length of only 19 squares. The other rows should each measure 23 squares in length.

Sew one of the short borders to each side of the pieced hearts. Press the seams open. Then sew long borders to the top and bottom of the pieced hearts, matching the seams at the corner intersections. Press the seams open.

Sew one 7 × 23½-inch white border to each side. Press the seams toward the borders. Sew a 7 × 36½-inch white border to the top and bottom. Press the seams toward the borders. See Diagram 7.

Spread out the 37-inch square of white fabric for the back. Place the square of batting on top of it, then spread the pieced top on top of the batting. Pin and baste all three layers together. Machine-stitch all around, ¼ inch from the outside edge. For instructions in quilt assembly see pages 18–26.

To Quilt

Set the wall hanging in the quilting frame and quilt in patterns as follows: Stitch ¼ inch around the outside of each heart. Use heart stencils for borders. Attach the red bias binding after you have finished quilting (see pages 24–26).

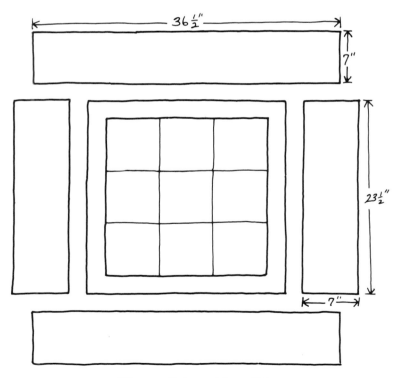

Diagram 7. Assemble quilt top.

Pillow

Make a companion pillow for the Holiday Hearts Wall Hanging. This most pleasing design is very easy to make.

MATERIALS

Fabric for four red hearts

Three 14½-inch squares of white muslin for the top, lining, and backing

14½-inch square of batting

Freezer paper

Glue stick

SEWING INSTRUCTIONS

Using the freezer paper technique described in the Holiday Hearts Wall Hanging instructions, cut out and appliqué four hearts on one 14½-inch square of muslin. Arrange them with their points together around the center of the square. See Diagram 1.

Place the batting on one square of muslin. Place the appliquéd top on top of the batting. Pin all three layers together.

Stitch around the square, ⅛ inch from the outside edge. Hand-quilt (optional) ¼ inch around each heart.

Using the third square of muslin for backing, finish the pillow plain or with a trim (see page 32).

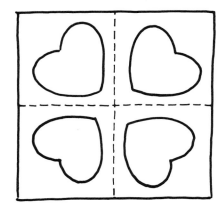

Diagram 1. Arrange hearts with points together around center of square.

Potholder

Make this quick and easy potholder using the heart design from the Holiday Hearts Wall Hanging.

MATERIALS

8-inch square of white fabric for top

Two 8-inch squares of batting for extra insulation

8-inch square of red or green fabric for back

1½ inches of ¼-inch red ribbon

1 yard of 2-inch bias trim to make ½-inch binding

Freezer paper

SEWING INSTRUCTIONS

Cut out and appliqué a heart to the center of the white square, using the freezer paper technique described in the instructions for the Holiday Hearts Wall Hanging (page 102).

Place the two squares of batting on the wrong side of the red or green backing square. Place the appliquéd white square on top of the batting with the heart right side up. Pin all four layers together.

Stitch all around the square, ⅛ inch from the outside edge. Pin a loop of ¼-inch red ribbon to one corner. See Diagram 1. Finish with 2-inch-wide bias trim to make a ½-inch-wide binding. See Binding the Quilt, page 24.

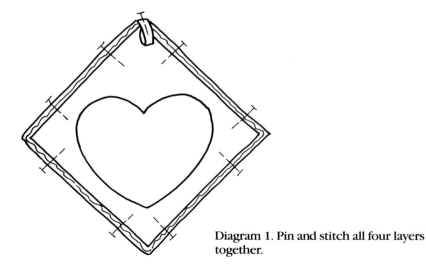

Diagram 1. Pin and stitch all four layers together.

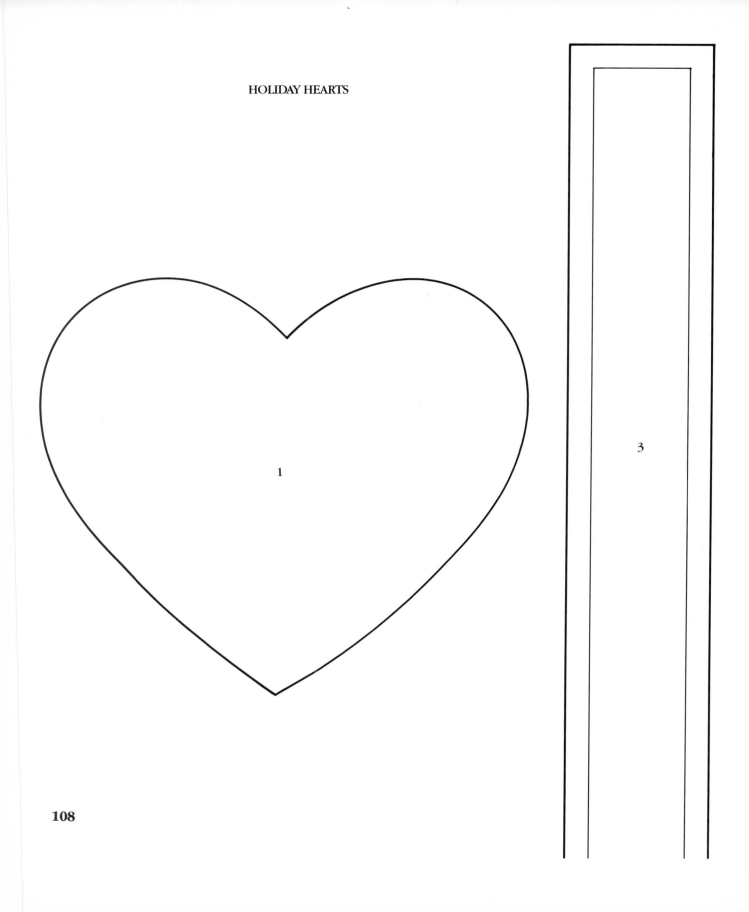

1

3

2

FOOD STUFFS

Most of the fruit and vegetable designs in this chapter are quite simple to make, and the sewing techniques vary little from one design to another. Those projects with the fewest number of pieces are the easiest to complete, so I would recommend starting with the Apple and other designs in its group (Summer Squash, Cucumber, Carrot, and Eggplant).

I have divided the instructions into groups according to the number of pieces required to make each fruit or vegetable. For example, because there is a strong similarity in construction among the Apple and the other items in its group (constructed from four pattern pieces), instructions and diagrams will be given for the Apple only. Other designs are made using five pattern pieces, some require six and so on. Instructions for those fruits and vegetables which require special parts or techniques (Corn, Banana, and Pineapple) can be found at the end of this chapter along with directions for making a Colonial Apple Cone.

BASIC SEWING TECHNIQUES FOR FRUITS AND VEGETABLES

In projects requiring multiples of the same pattern piece, cutting goes more quickly if you pin and cut from four layers of fabric at one time.

Fold the fabric in half, with right sides facing, and then fold it in half again. Pin the patterns in place or trace them with a pencil or fabric marker. For best results, use very sharp scissors to cut out the fabric shapes.

All of the pattern pieces include ¼-inch seam allowances. Start and end the seams ¼ inch from each edge unless otherwise specified. Do not stitch through the seam allowances. Backstitch at the beginning and end of each seam for extra strength.

To turn the fruits and vegetables right side out, leave a 1½-inch opening where indicated. Stuff each fruit or vegetable with polyester stuffing. Pin the openings and whipstitch them closed by hand.

Leaves and Stems

Many of the fruits and vegetables have leaves and stems. The stems are made with loops of ¼-inch green satin ribbon which can be used to attach the projects to Christmas trees, babies' cribs, or gift-wrapped packages.

The leaves shown are made from felt. If you plan to use the projects as toys for small children and will launder them often, cut the leaves from green calico instead of felt, and edge them with a zigzag stitch. Cut the stems from green grosgrain ribbon. Cotton calico fabric and grosgrain ribbon will hold up better than felt and satin under repeated washing and handling.

To save time, cut out a number of leaves and stems to have ready when you are preparing to sew the fruits and vegetables.

To assemble the stems and leaves: Fold a 1½-inch length of ¼-inch ribbon in half to make a loop. Tuck the loop in the center of a leaf, with the ends of the ribbon loop held against the base of the leaf. Fold the leaf over the stem, pin them together and place them on the fruit or vegetable as indicated in the instructions. See Diagram 1.

There are two different sizes for the basic leaf pattern. There are also special leaf patterns for the Eggplant, Tomato, and Pineapple. One or more leaves can be used on each fruit or vegetable.

Carrot and Turnip Tops

Each Carrot and Turnip top requires 30 inches of green satin cord (also known as "rat-tail"). Fold the cord into three 5-inch loops and stitch the ends together to hold them in place. Pin and stitch the looped tops in place where indicated in the instructions for the Carrot or the Turnip.

Woody Stems

There are patterns for woody stems in three different sizes. For each woody stem, cut four pieces from beige, green, or brown calico.

Starting ¼ inch from the top of the stem pieces, sew two pieces together (right sides together) along one side and continue stitching to the bottom edge. See Diagram 2. Repeat for a second pair of stem pieces. Trim the seams.

Pin and stitch the two sections together, with right sides together, matching the seams at the center-top. See Diagram 3. Clip the excess seam allowance at the center-top and turn the stem right side out.

Turn the raw edges under ¼ inch and pin. See Diagram 4. Stuff the stem as much as possible and pin it in place at the center-top of the fruit or vegetable (Pumpkin, Butternut Squash, etc.). Sew the stem in place by hand.

Diagram 1. Tuck ribbon loop stem inside leaf and pin.

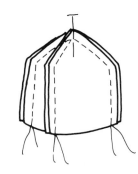

Diagram 2. Stitch two stem pieces together.

Diagram 3. Assemble stem.

Diagram 4. Pin under raw edges and sew stem in place.

113

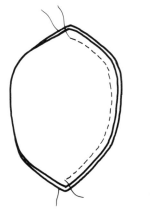

Diagram 1. Stitch two pieces together along one side.

Diagram 2. Pin leaf and ribbon loop to top of stem.

Four-Piece Designs: Apple, Summer Squash, Cucumber, Carrot, and Eggplant

The Apple has a leaf and a stem. The Summer Squash has a stem only. The Cucumber has neither. The Eggplant has its own leaf, and Carrot has its own top (page 113).

MATERIALS

Fabric
Red calico for Apple
Yellow calico for Summer Squash
Dark green calico for Cucumber
Orange calico for Carrot
Wine calico for Eggplant
Other Materials
Green felt or calico for leaves
¼-inch-wide green satin or grosgrain ribbon for stems
Green satin rat-tail cord for Carrot top
Polyester stuffing

SEWING INSTRUCTIONS

These instructions are for the Apple (the basic four-piece design); variations for the Carrot and Eggplant follow.

Cut four pieces from the specified fabrics for each design. With right sides together, sew two pieces together along one side. See Diagram 1. Repeat for the other two pieces.

Open out one section and pin a large leaf and a loop of ribbon for the stem to the right side at the center-top. See Diagram 2.

Open out the other section and pin it, right sides together, on top of the first section, matching the seams at the intersections. Rather than opening the seams at the intersections, finger-press them to one side of the seam. See Diagram 3.

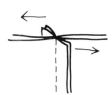

Diagram 3. Finger-press seam allowance to one side of seam.

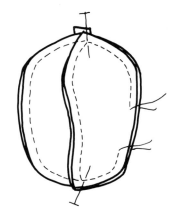

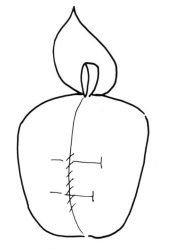

Diagram 4. Stitch halves together.

Diagram 5. Close opening by hand.

Sew the two halves together, catching the leaf and the stem at the center-top. Leave an opening along one side for turning. See Diagram 4.

Ease the seams at the intersections by clipping up to, but not through, the stitch lines at the center-top and center-bottom.

Remove the pins and turn right side out through the opening. Stuff, and close by hand. See Diagram 5.

Carrot

Instead of adding a leaf and a stem, pin the Carrot top of looped satin cord (page 113) to the right side of the fabric at the center-top of one section. Proceed to assemble as for the Apple.

Note: To make a sharp point at the tip of the Carrot, sew carefully to within ¼ inch of the end and stop with the needle down exactly at the point where the seams meet. Lift the presser foot and pivot the fabric. Continue sewing along the next side. To eliminate bulk, trim the seams and clip the excess seam allowance at the point.

Eggplant

Sew one Eggplant leaf to the right side of each of the four Eggplant pieces. See Diagram 6. Proceed to assemble as for the Apple, using only a stem at the center-top.

Diagram 6. Sew eggplant leaf to each eggplant piece.

Five-Piece Designs: Pear, Orange, Turnip, and Gourd (shown on page 118)

The Pear and the Orange have leaves and stems. The Turnip has a piece of white cord on the bottom. The Gourd does not have a leaf or stem.

MATERIALS

Fabric

Yellow or green calico for Pear

Orange calico for Orange

White cotton and lavender calico for Turnip

Yellow calico and green calico for Gourd

Other Materials

Green felt or calico for leaves

¼-inch green satin or grosgrain ribbon for stems

White cord for Turnip

Polyester stuffing

SEWING INSTRUCTIONS

Cut five pieces from the specified fabrics for the Pear and the Orange.

For the Turnip, cut one 3½ × 15-inch strip of white cotton and one of lavender calico. Stitch the long sides together. Press the seam open. Place the Turnip pattern on the fabric so that the top is on the lavender and the bottom is on the white. See Diagram 1. Cut out five pattern pieces and assemble as for the Pear, matching the seams at the intersections between the lavender and the white.

For the Gourd, cut a 2½ × 8¾-inch strip of yellow calico and a 3½ × 8¾-inch strip of green. Sew them together, press the seam open and proceed as for the Turnip.

With right sides facing, sew two pieces together along one side. Repeat for two more pieces.

Pin and stitch the fifth piece to one side of one of the two-piece sections so the seams meet exactly at the center-top and center-bottom. See Diagram 2.

Open out the three-part section and pin a small folded leaf and a ribbon loop stem at the center-top (except for the Turnip and the Gourd). Open out the two-part section and pin it in place over the three-part section so that the seams meet at the intersections. Let the seam allowances lie to one side in opposite directions on the three-part section. See Diagram 3.

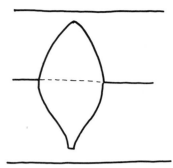

Diagram 1. Cut turnip from pieced lavender and white fabric.

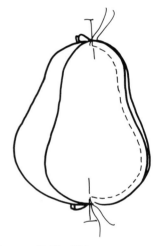

Diagram 2. Pin fifth piece in place, matching seams.

Diagram 3. Finger-press seams to opposite sides.

117

Sew the two sections together, catching the leaf and the stem in the seam at the center-top. Leave an opening on one side for turning. To ease tension at the intersections, clip the seams up to, but not through, the stitch lines of the intersections at the center-top and center-bottom.

Remove the pins and turn the fruit right side out through the opening. Stuff with polyester stuffing and close by hand.

Turnip

Optional: Before assembling the two sections, cut a 3-inch-long piece of white satin rat-tail cord and pin and stitch it in place at the center-bottom of the Turnip. To eliminate bulk, clip the seams and excess cord at the center-bottom before turning the Turnip right side out.

Six-Piece Designs: Grapefruit, Lemon, Lime, Tomato, Butternut Squash, and Lettuce or Red Cabbage (shown on page 121)

The Grapefruit has one large leaf and a stem. Eliminate the leaf for the Lemon and the Lime. The Tomato and the Lettuce or Red Cabbage each have their own leaves, and the Tomato also has a stem. The Butternut Squash has a small woody stem (page 113).

MATERIALS

Fabric
Yellow calico for Grapefruit
Yellow calico for Lemon
Bright green calico for Lime
Red calico for Tomato
Beige calico for Butternut Squash
Light green calico for Lettuce
Burgundy calico for Red Cabbage
Beige, green, or brown calico for woody stem on Butternut Squash

Other Materials
Green felt or calico for leaves
¼-inch green satin or grosgrain ribbon for stems
Polyester stuffing

SEWING INSTRUCTIONS

Cut six pieces from specified fabrics for each design. For Lettuce or Red Cabbage, cut six inner pieces and six outer leaves.

With right sides facing, sew two pieces together along one side. Repeat with two more pieces.

Open out one of the two-piece sections and pin one of the remaining pieces to its side so that the seams meet exactly at the center-top and center-bottom. Repeat for the other two-piece section and the remaining piece. See Diagram 1.

Open out one three-part section and pin one large folded leaf and a ribbon loop stem to the center-top. Open out the other three-part section and pin it in place over the first, matching the seams where they intersect at the top and the bottom. Let the seams lie to the sides, away from each other. See Diagram 2.

Sew the two sections together, catching the leaf and stem in the seam at the top, and leaving an opening on one side for turning. To ease the tension at the intersections, clip the seams up to, but not through, the stitch lines at the center-top and center-bottom.

Remove the pins and turn right side out through the opening. Stuff with polyester stuffing and close the opening by hand.

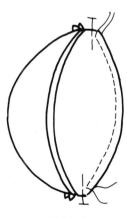

Diagram 1. Add third piece to each half.

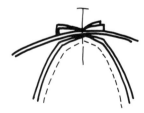

Diagram 2. Pin and stitch two halves together.

Diagram 3. Sew one leaf to each set of two tomato pieces.

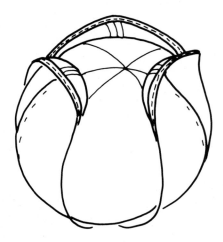

Diagram 4. Hand-stitch outer leaves in place.

Tomato

Although the Tomato has six pieces, it is assembled a little differently from other six-piece designs because each of its three leaves spans two pieces.

With right sides facing, sew two Tomato pieces together along one side. Repeat for two more pairs of pieces.

Cut three leaves, using the Tomato Leaf pattern, and sew one leaf in place over each pair of Tomato pieces. See Diagram 3.

Sew two sets together. Pin the ribbon loop stem at the center-top.

Pin and sew the third set of Tomato pieces along one side of the section completed above.

Sew the remaining two sides together in the same way, leaving an opening for turning. Turn the Tomato right side out. Stuff with polyester stuffing and close the opening by hand.

Lettuce or Red Cabbage

Assemble six pieces of inner Lettuce or Red Cabbage as for the other six-piece designs. With right sides facing fold leaf at the fold line, and stitch from one point, along fold, to point at other end. Repeat for all three outer leaves. Press the seams open.

Turn the edge under ⅛ inch and stitch around the entire curve on each outer leaf. Press around outside edge.

Wrap the outer leaves around the inner Lettuce or Red Cabbage so that their edges overlap and the center seams meet at the top and bottom. Pin the outer leaves in place. With a needle and thread, hand-tack each leaf to the Lettuce starting at the center-bottom and continuing up through the center seam of each outer leaf, stopping about 2 inches from the top. See Diagram 4.

Eight-Piece Design: Cherry Tomato

Fill a pint container from your local produce stand with calico Cherry Tomatoes.

MATERIALS

Fabric
Red calico

Other Materials
¼-inch-wide green satin or grosgrain ribbon for stems
Polyester stuffing

122

SEWING INSTRUCTIONS

Cut eight pattern pieces for each Cherry Tomato.

To facilitate sewing around small curves, shorten the stitch length on the sewing machine. Starting at the very edge of one seam line, sew two pieces together along one side, right sides facing. Do not start and stop ¼ inch from each end, as with other designs, but stitch right off the edge and then slip the next piece under the presser foot and continue stitching. See Diagram 1.

Repeat for a total of four sets of two pieces each. See Assembly-Line Piecing, page 17. Clip the threads between each set and trim the seam allowance.

Pin and sew two sets of pieces together along one side to make a half-ball, matching the seams at the intersections. See Diagram 2. Finger-press the seams to lie in opposite directions. Repeat for the remaining two sets of pieces. Trim the seam allowance.

Pin the two half-ball sections together and pin a ribbon loop stem at one intersection. Starting just before one intersection, stitch the two halves together, ending just beyond the last intersection. See Diagram 3. Leave an opening between the two intersections for turning.

Trim the seam allowance. Turn the Cherry Tomato right side out through the opening. Stuff with polyester stuffing and close the opening by hand.

Ten-Piece Designs: Round Gourd and Blue Moon Squash

The Round Gourd has a ribbon loop stem and the Blue Moon Squash has a small woody stem. The patterns for the Round Gourd are given in both small and large sizes.

MATERIALS

Fabric

Green calico and yellow calico, *or* green calico and white calico, *or* rust calico and yellow calico for Round Gourd

Pale blue calico for Blue Moon Squash

Green, brown, or beige calico for woody stem on Blue Moon Squash

Other Materials

¼-inch-wide green satin or grosgrain ribbon for stem

Polyester stuffing

Diagram 1. Stitch pieces together, using assembly-line technique.

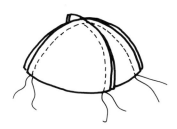

Diagram 2. Sew four pattern pieces together to make half ball.

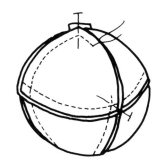

Diagram 3. Pin and stitch two halves together.

SEWING INSTRUCTIONS

The Round Gourd is made with two different-colored fabrics. Cut five pieces each of either green and yellow calicos, green and white calicos, or rust and yellow calicos for each Round Gourd. Cut ten pieces of pale blue calico for the Blue Moon Squash.

With right sides together, sew two pieces together along one side. For the Round Gourd, sew two different colors together. Repeat to make a total of four sets of two pieces each. You will have two single pieces left over.

Pin two sets together so that the seams meet exactly at the center-top and the center-bottom. Sew, stopping and starting ¼ inch from the top and bottom. Repeat for the remaining two sets.

Next, pin one of the single pieces to one side of one of the sections you just completed, and stitch it in place. Repeat to complete two sections of five pieces each. Because there are so many pieces, be especially careful to match the seams so that they all meet neatly at the top and bottom.

Pin both of the two five-piece sections together with a ribbon loop stem at the center-top (omit for Blue Moon Squash), matching the seams at the center-top and the center-bottom. Sew the two sections together, catching the stem in the seam at the top, and leaving an opening on one side for turning.

To ease the tension at the intersections, clip the seams up to, but not through, the stitch lines at the center-top and center-bottom.

Remove the pins and turn the design right side out through the opening. Stuff with polyester stuffing and close the opening by hand.

For the Blue Moon Squash, pin a small woody stem (page 113) to the center-top and attach by hand.

Fourteen-Piece Design: Pumpkin

There are patterns for the Pumpkin in two sizes, small and large.

MATERIALS

Fabric
Orange calico for Pumpkin
Beige calico for woody stem

SEWING INSTRUCTIONS

Cut fourteen pieces from orange calico for each Pumpkin. Cut four pieces from beige calico for each woody stem.

The Pumpkin is made exactly the same way as the Round Gourd, except that it has fourteen pieces instead of ten. Sew these pieces together as for the Round Gourd, creating two sections of *seven* pieces each.

Because the top of the pattern is smaller than the bottom, the notches

indicate which ends go together. Carefully match the seams so that they all meet neatly at the center-top and at the center-bottom.

Attach a small or a large woody stem to the center-top of the small or large Pumpkin respectively.

Corn

The Corn is made in two separate parts: the Corn Cob and the Corn Husk.

MATERIALS

Fabric

Yellow calico or small yellow and white gingham check for Corn Cob

Light green calico for Corn Husk

Other Materials

Polyester stuffing

SEWING INSTRUCTIONS

Cut three pieces for each Corn Cob. Cut four pieces for the Corn Husk.

With right sides facing, sew two Corn Cob pieces together along one side. See Diagram 1.

Pin and stitch the third piece to one side of the section just completed, matching the seams at the center-top and the center-bottom.

Sew the remaining two sides together in the same way, leaving an opening for turning.

Clip the excess seam allowance at the center-top and bottom corners and turn the Corn Cob right side out through the opening. Stuff with polyester stuffing and whipstitch the opening closed by hand.

Each ear of Corn has two husk leaves, each made with two pieces.

With right sides facing, sew two husk pieces together, leaving an opening on the bottom end of one side. Repeat for the second husk. To eliminate bulk, clip excess seam allowance at center-top and side corners. See Diagram 2.

Turn the husk leaves right side out through the openings. Turn the raw edges of the opening to the inside. Press husks. Whipstitch the openings closed.

Fold one husk leaf in half lengthwise and stitch the dart as indicated on the pattern. Repeat for the second husk.

Sew the two leaves together by hand, stitching along the bottom around the corner and continuing about two inches up one side. See Diagram 3.

Fold the leaves around the Corn Cob with the darts on the inside. Tack the leaves in place on the Corn Cob where the husks meet each other at the front and back.

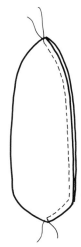

Diagram 1. Sew two Corn Cob pieces together along one side.

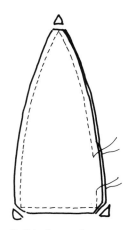

Diagram 2. Stitch two leaves together; trim seams.

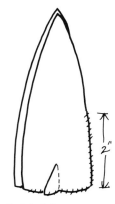

Diagram 3. Stitch leaves together along bottom and part way up one side.

129

Banana

The Banana has three different pattern pieces with notches as guides for joining the seams.

MATERIALS

Fabric

Yellow calico

Pattern piece	Number of pieces
1	1
2	2
3	2

SEWING INSTRUCTIONS

Note: It will not be necessary to begin and end exactly ¼ inch from the edge of each seam. Begin and end all seams right at the edge of the fabric.

With right sides together, pin one piece #2 to one side of piece #1, matching all of the notches. Before stitching, clip the seam up to, but not through, the stitch line on piece #2. Clip at the corner near the stem and every ½ inch along the curve. This will ease the curve, making the pieces easier to join. Pin often and adjust the fullness where necessary to ease the seam on piece #2 to fit piece #1. Baste (optional) and sew. Join the other piece #2 to the other side of piece #1 in the same way. Remove the pins. See Diagram 1.

With right sides facing, pin one piece #3 to one piece #2, carefully matching the notches. Clip the seam allowance up to, but not through, the stitch line about every ½ inch to ease the curve. Pin the seam often and adjust where necessary, easing to fit. Baste (optional) and sew. Repeat for the second #3 piece. Remove the pins.

Sew the bottom sides (where there are three notches) of the two #3 pieces together, leaving an opening in the middle of the seam for turning.

Trim the seam allowance on all of the seams. Sew over the ends of the stem and the bottom end of the Banana, and clip the excess seam allowance to eliminate bulk. Turn the Banana right side out, stuff, and whipstitch the opening closed.

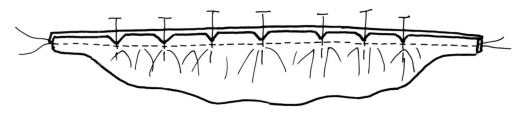

Diagram 1. Join one piece #2 to either side of piece #1.

Pineapple

The Pineapple, symbol of hospitality, can stand alone or serve as the focal point of the Colonial Apple Cone (page 132).

MATERIALS

Fabric

Beige, yellow, brown, or orange print fabric (with a diamond motif if possible)

Other Materials

Fabric glue

¼ yard of green felt for leaves

Spool of green twist-tie wire (for twist-tie dispensers) or florist's wire

Narrow cotton cord

3-inch length of 2-inch-diameter mailing tube

Green felt-tip marker

Polyester stuffing

SEWING INSTRUCTIONS

Cut four pattern pieces for each Pineapple.

Sew two pieces together along one side, with right sides facing. Repeat for the other two pieces.

Sew these two sections together, matching the seams at the point and leaving the large end open.

Fold the top edge of the open end under ¼ inch and stitch around the entire edge. Fold the edge over again ½ inch and stitch down ½ inch from the top to make a narrow casing for the drawstring. Leave a small opening to insert the drawstring. See Diagram 1.

Attach a safety pin or paper clip to one end of a piece of narrow cotton cord. Insert the cord into the casing and pull the cord through to the other end.

Turn the Pineapple right side out and stuff with polyester stuffing. Pull the drawstring tight to close the opening and tie it off after inserting the Pineapple Leaves. See Diagram 2.

Pineapple Leaves

For each Pineapple, cut three rows of leaves, in three lengths, from green felt.

Cut eight each of 4½-inch, 6½-inch and 8½-inch lengths of twist-tie wire for the small, medium, and large leaves respectively.

Squeeze out a thin line of glue down the length of one short twist-tie. Place

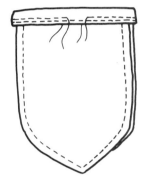

Diagram 1. Make casing for drawstring.

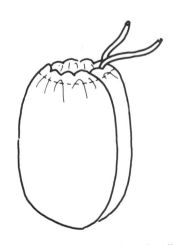

Diagram 2. Stuff Pineapple and pull drawstring.

133

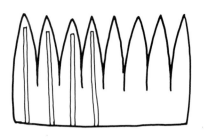

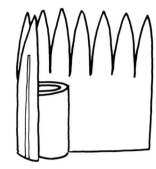

Diagram 3. Glue a twist-tie wire to center of each leaf.

Diagram 4. Glue leaves around outside of small cardboard tube.

it on the center of one small leaf and press it down with your fingertip. Repeat for each leaf. Allow the glue to dry thoroughly. See Diagram 3.

Color the top and the inside of the 3-inch piece of mailing tube with the green marker. Glue the largest set of leaves to the outside of the tube (twist-ties facing out) so both edges meet. See Diagram 4.

Starting and ending in a different place, glue the medium-sized set of leaves on top of the first, matching the base lines. Because of the added thickness, stretch the leaves a little when you wrap them so that both ends meet.

Glue the third and smallest set of leaves around the tube on top of the medium-sized leaves, stretching the leaves a little when you wrap them around. Allow the glue to dry thoroughly.

Insert the finished Pineapple Leaves into the top of the Pineapple. Pull the drawstring over the bottom edge of the tube and tie it tightly. Tuck the ends of the cord inside. By hand, slipstitch the top edge of the Pineapple to the felt on the bottom edge of the tube. Gently shape the leaves so that they bend gracefully over the Pineapple.

Colonial Apple Cone   (shown on page 132)

Colonial apple cones, or fruit pyramids, have long been a tradition in this country. Decorated with apples or pears and topped with a pineapple, they create quite a dramatic centerpiece on a holiday table or sideboard. A calico pineapple surrounded by calico pears or apples substituting for the real thing will add a touch of gaiety and humor to your holiday festivities.

MATERIALS

1 Pineapple (page 133)
12 Apples (page 114) or Pears (page 117)
9-inch apple cone (See Source List on page 9
   for merchandise information.)

33 sewing machine needles

8 to 10 large artificial green leaves

**About 1 dozen stems with clusters of small
artificial green leaves**

Staple gun

Pliers

INSTRUCTIONS

Pull the nails out of the apple cone with pliers.

Staple the large artificial leaves to the underside of the apple cone so that they fan out from the base.

Insert the large end of a sewing machine needle in each nail hole. Secure with a dab of white glue, if desired.

Distributing the leaves evenly, arrange the stems of small leaves in place around the apple cone. Trim the stems if necessary, and staple them in place.

Place the Pineapple on the needles on top of the apple cone. Arrange Pears or Apples evenly in two tiers around the sides of the cone.

FOOD STUFFS

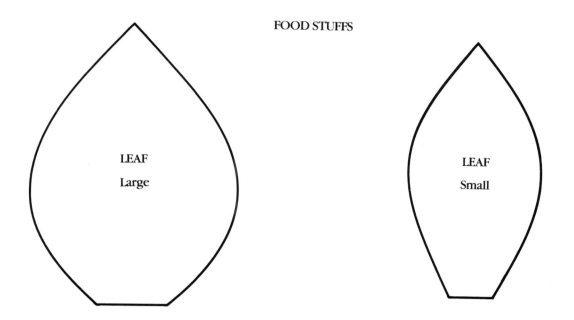

LEAF
Large

LEAF
Small

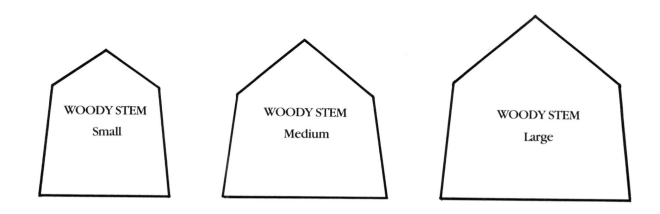

WOODY STEM
Small

WOODY STEM
Medium

WOODY STEM
Large

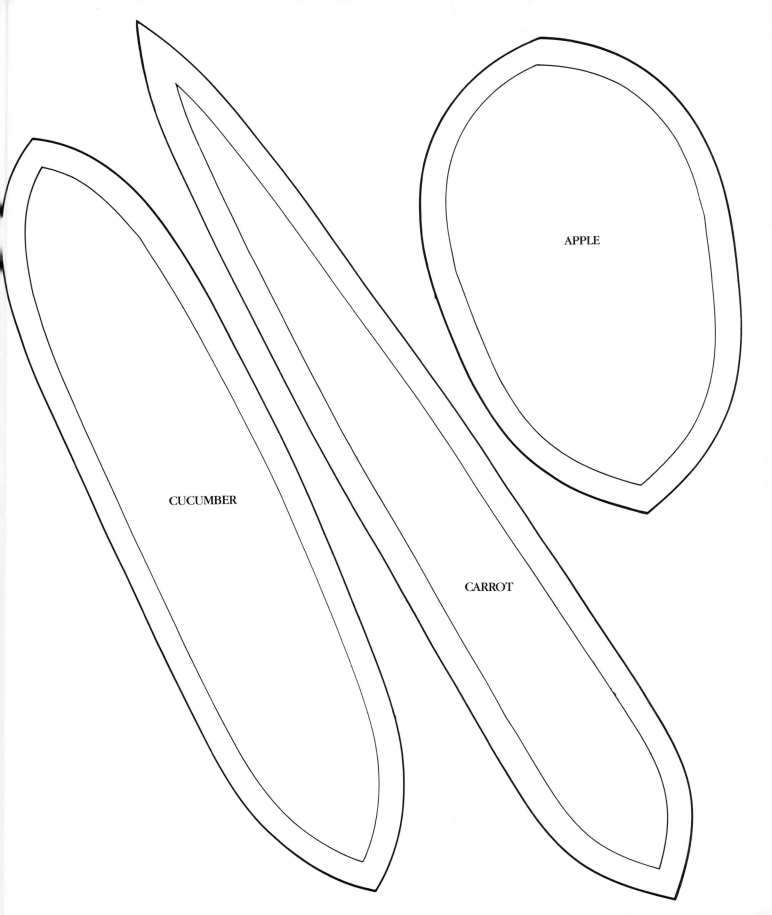

CUCUMBER

CARROT

APPLE

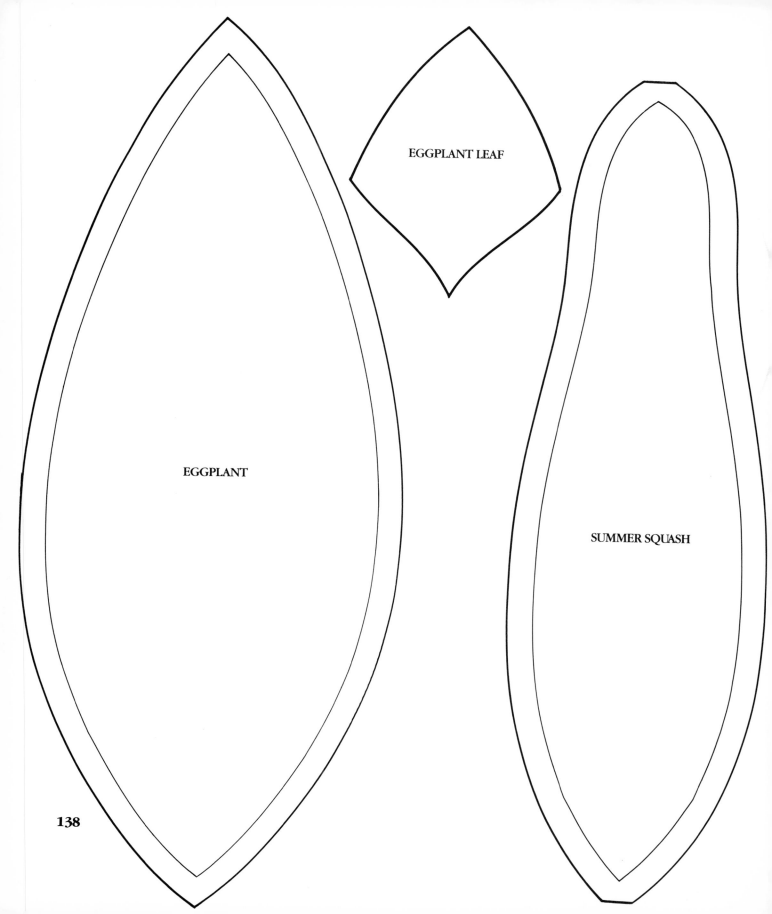

EGGPLANT LEAF

EGGPLANT

SUMMER SQUASH

138

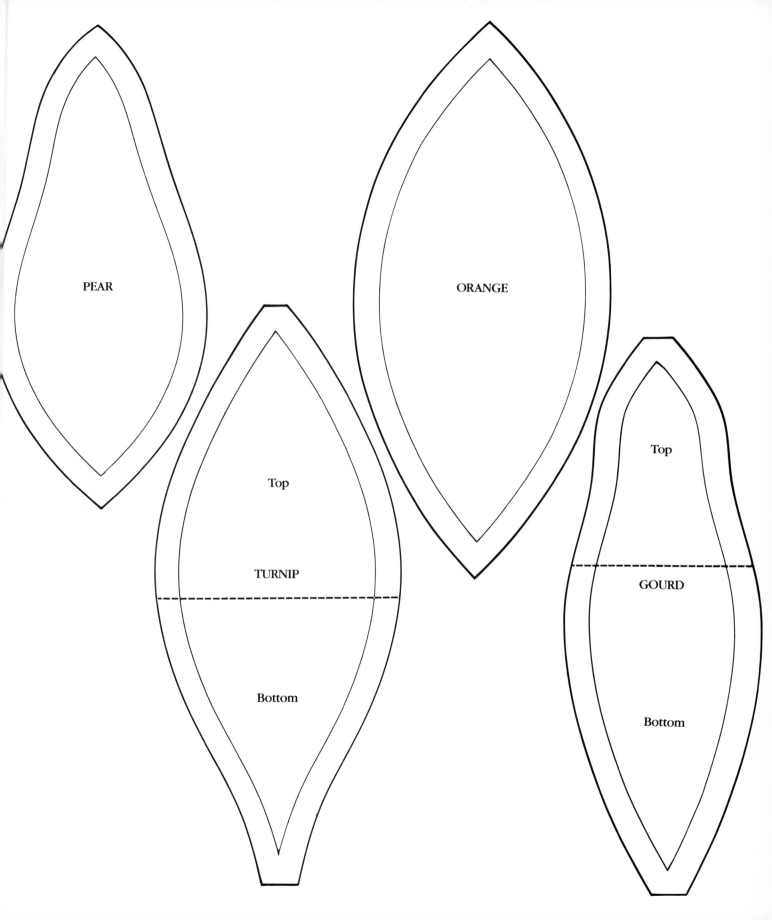

PEAR

ORANGE

Top

TURNIP

Bottom

Top

GOURD

Bottom

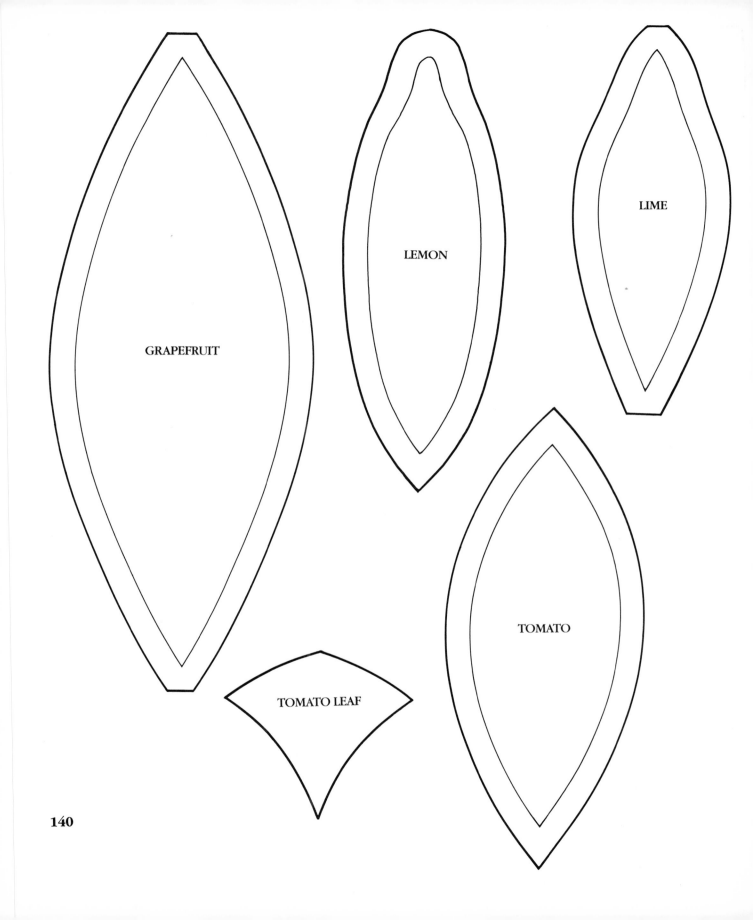

GRAPEFRUIT

LEMON

LIME

TOMATO

TOMATO LEAF

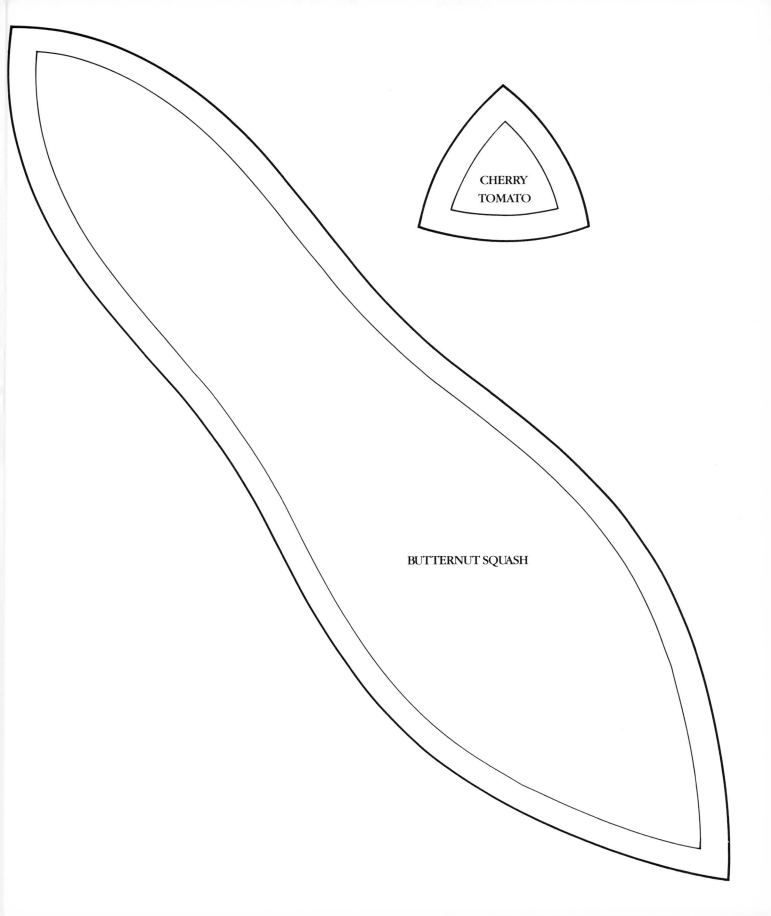

CHERRY
TOMATO

BUTTERNUT SQUASH

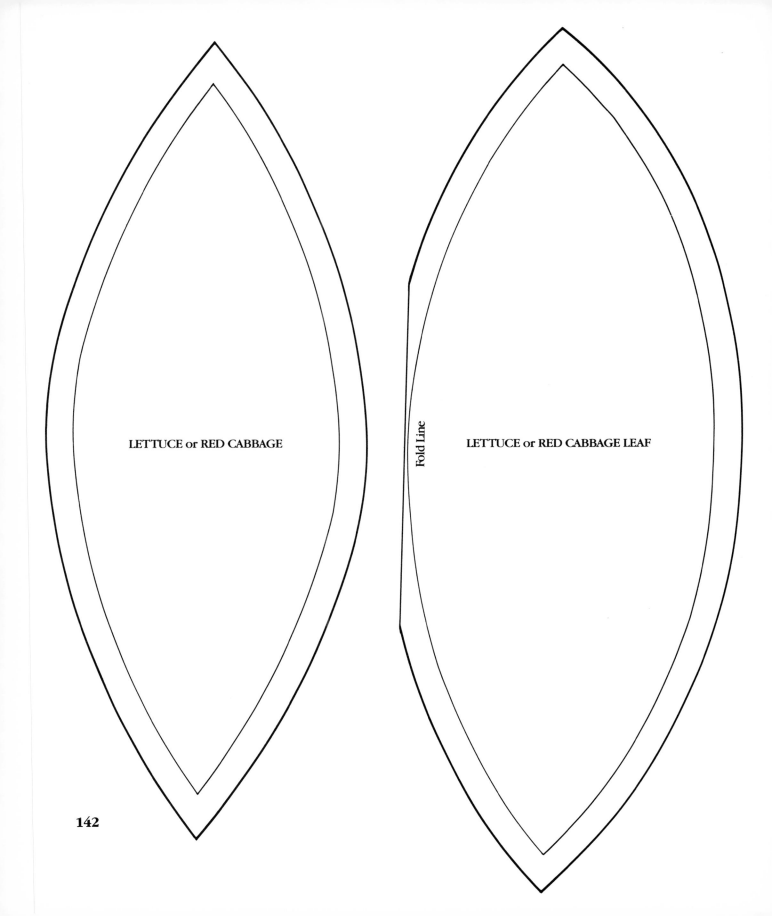

LETTUCE or RED CABBAGE

Fold Line

LETTUCE or RED CABBAGE LEAF

142

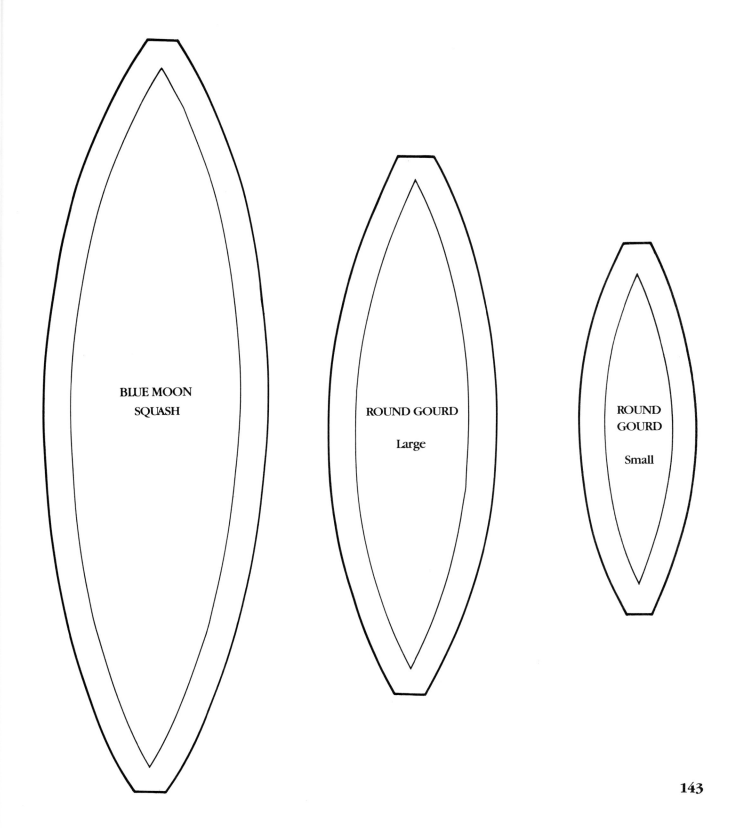

BLUE MOON
SQUASH

ROUND GOURD

Large

ROUND
GOURD

Small

143

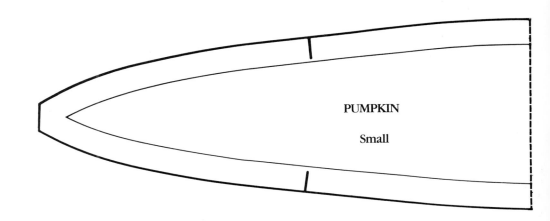

PUMPKIN

Small

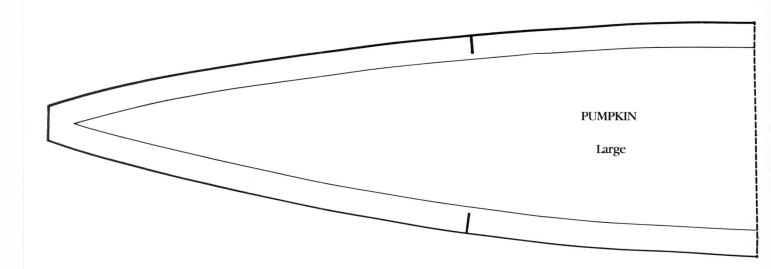

PUMPKIN

Large

144

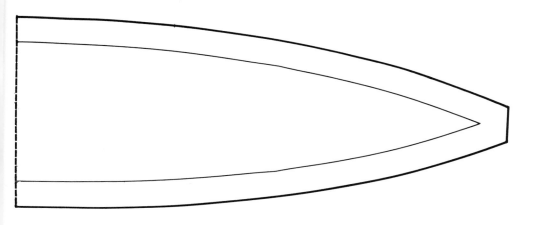

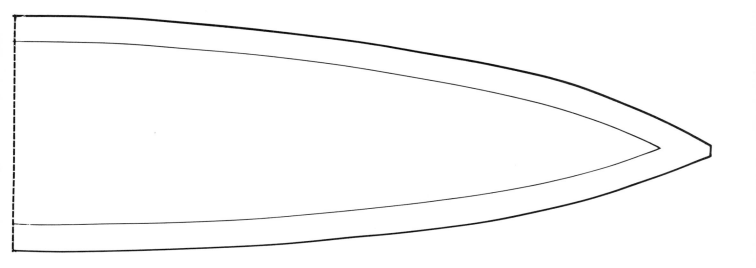

145

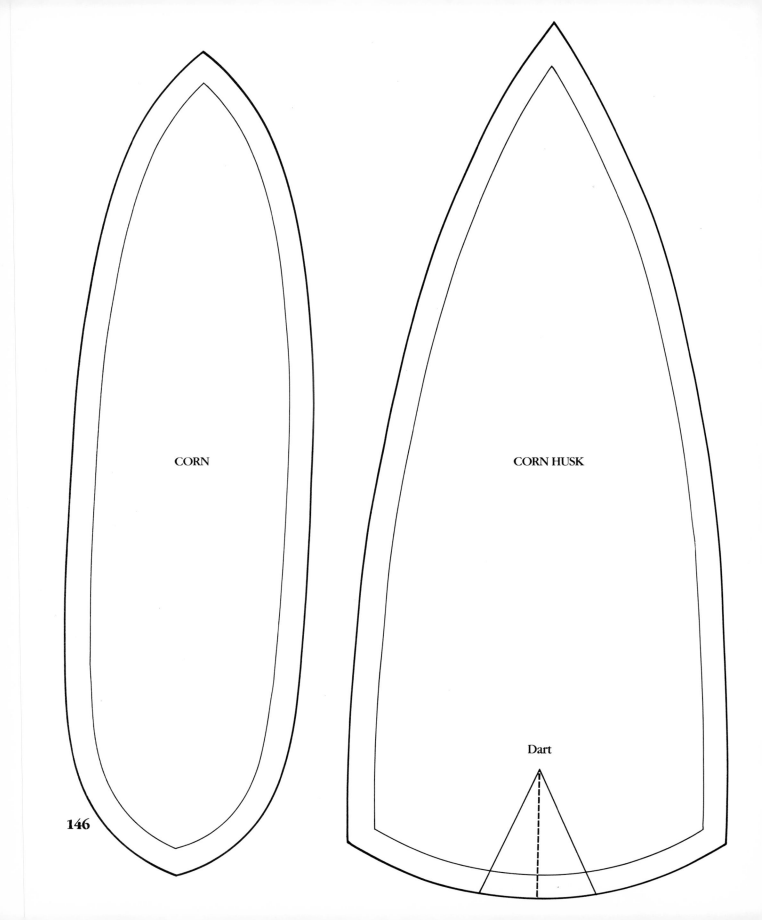

CORN

CORN HUSK

Dart

146

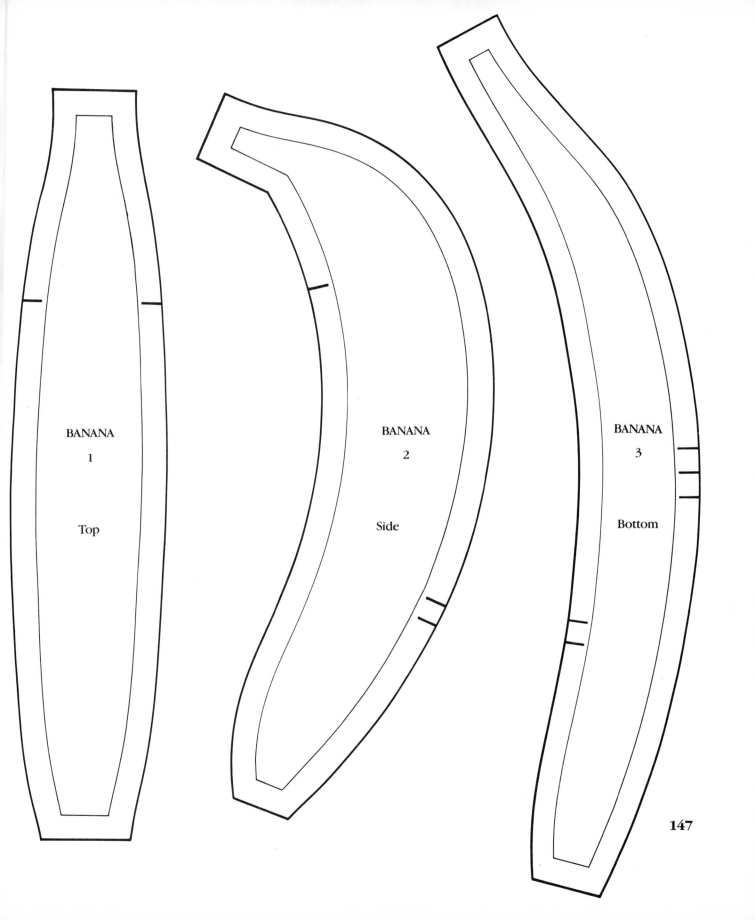

BANANA

1

Top

BANANA

2

Side

BANANA

3

Bottom

147

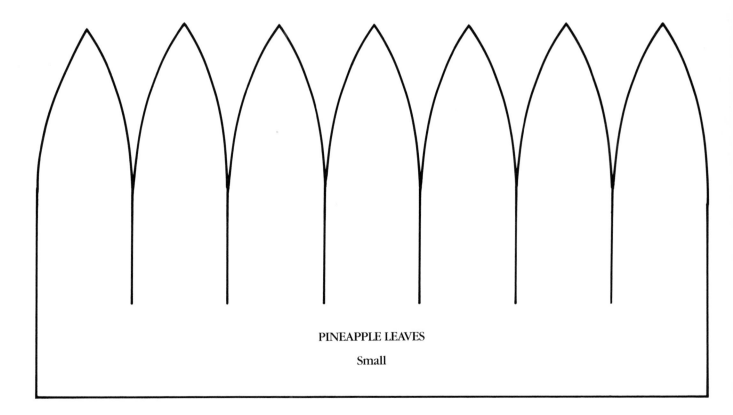

PINEAPPLE LEAVES

Small

148

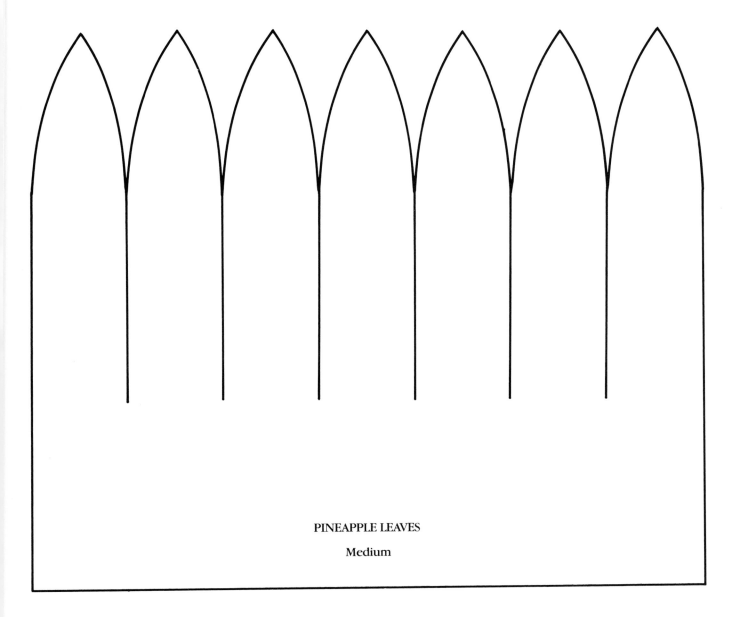

PINEAPPLE LEAVES

Medium

149

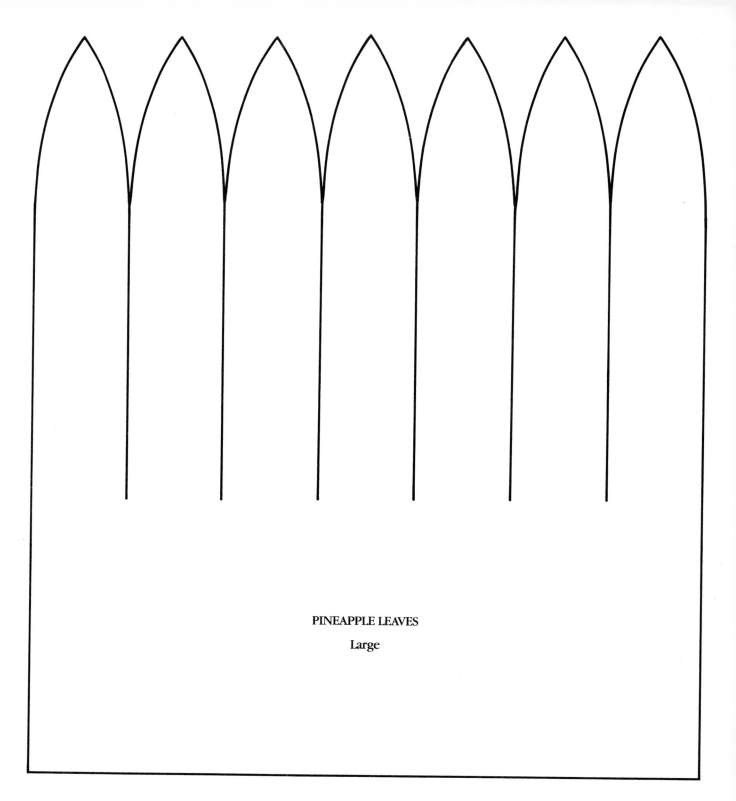

PINEAPPLE LEAVES

Large

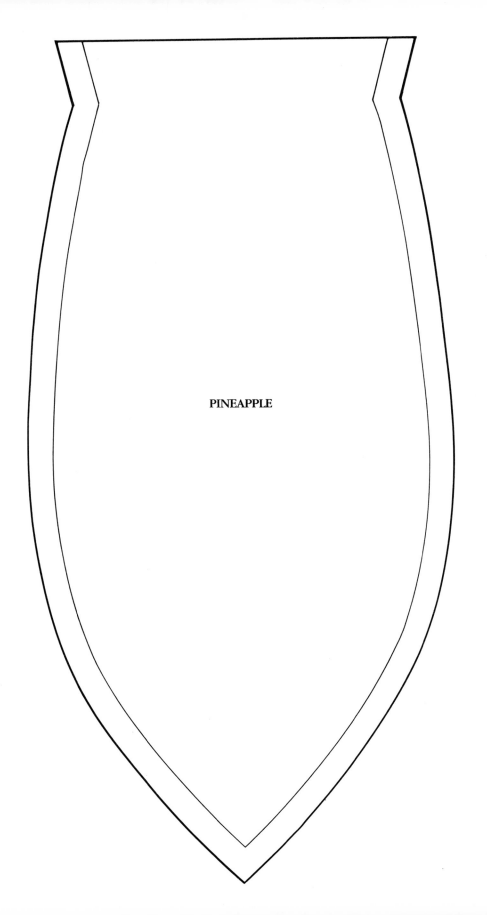

PINEAPPLE

151

CHRISTMAS TREES AND FEATHERED STARS

The designs in this chapter are directly related to one another. Each is made of different combinations of the patterns found at the end of this section. Since all of the designs in this chapter share the same patterns, making one is, in a way, preparation for the next.

The first design, Whirling Pine, is the easiest to make. It consists of a simple tree shape (derived from a traditional patchwork pattern called Spider Web) to which I have added a square base to suggest a tree trunk. The overall square, or circular, design is divided into eight equal parts. One tree is exactly ⅛ of a circle. See Diagram 1.

This simple tree design provides the basic structure for the slightly more complex Christmas Pine design which begins with the same three pattern pieces. The "branches" of the Christmas Pine — actually squares composed of two different-colored right triangles — are added to the sides of the trees and completed with a diamond at the top. Here again, one pieced tree is equal to ⅛ of a circle, and eight trees make one circle or square. See Diagram 2.

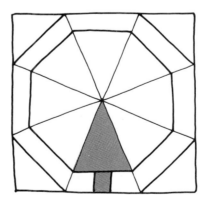

Diagram 1. Whirling Pine design.   Diagram 2. Christmas Pine design.

Diagram 3. Treetops pointing into center.

Diagram 4. Treetops pointing away from center.

The trees can be arranged in a circle with their tops meeting at the center (page 153). Or they can be arranged in rows, as in the Christmas Pine Quilt (page 165). They can also radiate outward, as in the Star and Pine Quilt (page 168). See Diagram 4.

The space created in the center of the Star and Pine design becomes an eight-pointed star. The interesting thing about this design is that the diamond-shaped block containing both the tree and ⅛ of the star is exactly the same size as the diamond in the Simple Feathered Star and the Feathered Star. See Diagram 5.

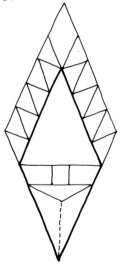

Diagram 5.

Star and Pine.

Simple Feathered Star.

155

Diagram 6. Feathered Star.

You can also see that the "branches" of the Christmas Pine and the Star and Pine designs are the same as the "feathers" of the Simple Feathered Star and Feathered Star designs. This is why the patterns for these designs are interchangeable.

Ambitious quilters may want to go still further. Instead of making a Simple Feathered Star, you may choose to subdivide the diamond into smaller pieces for the more complex sixteen-piece diamond in the Feathered Star design. See Diagram 6.

All sixteen diamonds can be used to create a design, or you might use any combination of two or more of the sixteen parts to create a pattern-within-a-pattern in the diamond. See Diagram 7.

By varying the colors and arrangements of these basic shapes any number of interesting designs can be created. Striped fabric, for example, takes on an added dimension when you use the stripes to create strong directional accents. See photos on pages 180–181.

When you make a Simple Feathered Star or a Feathered Star quilt, all of the stars can be the same, or each star can be different. I find it more interesting to work on a quilt if there is some variation among the quilt blocks. How it's done is really a matter of personal preference.

The designs in this chapter range from the very simple to the very complex. Beginners and those with limited quilting experience may want to start with the Whirling Pine and progress to the Christmas Pine. Smaller projects give the beginner a chance to experience the pleasure of working out a given design without being overwhelmed. Making a pillow to start is a good way to get the feel for piecing and quilting.

Once you feel comfortable with these techniques you can begin to move on through the chapter to the larger or more complicated projects.

Experienced quilters may want to dive right in. You will find the Feathered Star Quilt to be a challenging but satisfying endeavor.

Diagram 7. Possible pattern variations.

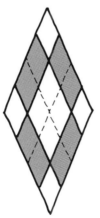 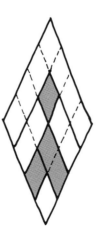 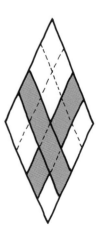

Whirling Pine (shown on page 153)

The Whirling Pine block is made of eight trees arranged in a circle with their tops meeting at the center. The block is appropriate as a pillow top or, in groups, as a quilt top.

MATERIALS

Fabric

Pattern piece	Number of pieces
1	8
2	8
3	16
4	4

Other Materials

For a pillow:

10-inch zipper

12-inch square of backing fabric

12-inch square pillow form

For a quilt composed of nine blocks:

60-inch square of batting

3⅓ yards of 36-inch or 48-inch backing fabric

4½ yards of 1½-inch trim to make a 1-inch inner border

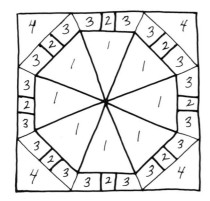 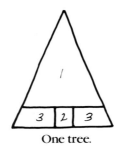

One tree.

Piecing diagrams.

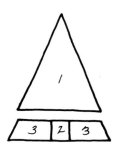

Diagram 1. Stitch one #3 to each side of a #2.

SEWING INSTRUCTIONS

Cut out and sew one piece #3 to one side of each piece #2. Press the seams open. Sew a #3 to the other side of each #2. Press the seams open.

Sew a piece #1 to the top of each 2-3 section completed above. See Diagram 1. Press the seams open.

Sew two of the completed trees together along one side. Repeat for four pairs of trees. Press the seams open. See Diagram 2.

Sew two pairs of trees together in the same way. Repeat for the other two pairs of trees. Press the seams open. See Diagram 3.

Sew the two halves of the block together, matching the seams at the center and the intersections. Press the seams open.

Sew one triangle (piece #4) to the bottom of every other tree to create a square. Press the seams toward the corners. See piecing diagram.

To assemble the pillow see page 33.

Quilt Top

Any number of Whirling Pine blocks can be assembled into a quilt top. The following directions are for a quilt with nine 12-inch-square blocks.

Make nine blocks following the directions above. Sew three blocks together in a row. Repeat for a total of three rows. Press the seams open.

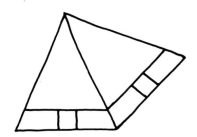

Diagram 2. Sew two trees together.

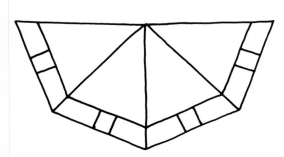

Diagram 3. Sew two pairs of trees together to make one-half design.

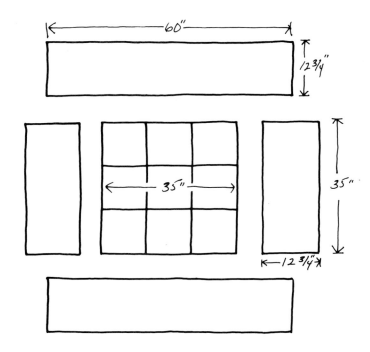

Diagram 4. Add borders to pieced quilt top.

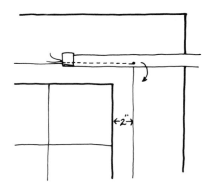
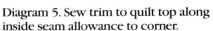
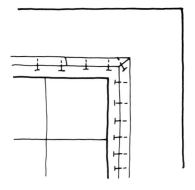

Diagram 5. Sew trim to quilt top along
inside seam allowance to corner.

Diagram 6. Fold trim over, tuck under
seam allowance, miter corners.

Sew the rows together to create a square of three blocks across and three down. Carefully match all of the seams at the intersections. Press the seams open.

Sew a 12¾ × 35-inch border to each side of the quilt. Press the seams to one side toward the borders. Now, sew a 12¾ × 60-inch border to the quilt top and bottom. See Diagram 4. Press the seams toward the borders.

Optional: A piece of 1-inch trim can be added as an accent on the border around the trees, picking up one of the colors in the quilt.

Fold under each edge of the 1½-inch trim ¼ inch and press.

Mark a line (with pencil or removable marker) around each side of the border of the quilt top 2 inches from the tree area.

Right sides together, place the trim on the border on one side of the quilt top (not at a corner) with the inside seam allowance on the line marked on the quilt top. Fold over the end of the trim ¼ inch. Machine-stitch the trim to the quilt top up to the corner. See Diagram 5.

Leave the needle down at the corner, lift the presser foot, pivot and adjust the quilt top. To turn the corner neatly without any puckers, stretch the trim firmly around the corner (the trim will wrap around the presser foot) and line it up with the inside seam allowance on the line marked on the next border. Lower the presser foot and continue sewing up to the next corner. Repeat for each corner.

To finish, sew the trim over the first end ¼ inch, remove from the sewing machine and cut.

Tucking under the seam allowance on the other edge of the trim, fold the trim over and press it toward the center of the quilt top, folding and mitering the corners. See Diagram 6. Pin the trim in place and whipstitch the edge to the quilt top.

See instructions for assembling and finishing (pages 18–26).

Christmas Pine Pillow (shown on page 153)

Just as for the Whirling Pine, eight pieced Christmas Pines will make a pillow top, thirty-two or more will make a quilt with four or more blocks. The Christmas Pine has "branches" constructed exactly the same way as the "feathers" in the Feathered Star (page 180).

The following instructions are for eight Christmas Pines, which, when sewn together, will make one pillow top.

MATERIALS

Fabric

Pattern piece	Number of pieces
1	8 green
2	8 green
3	16 white
5	64 green, 80 white
6	16 white
7	8 green
8	4 white

Note: Not all of the trees have to be the same shade of green. A darker or lighter green can be used for half of them, or use a different color altogether. If this is to be the case, divide the number of green pieces in the cutting chart in half for both colors.

CUTTING BRANCHES

The following instructions pertain to cutting "branches" or "feathers" for all Christmas Pine and Feathered Star designs. When cutting for any of the Feathered Star designs, substitute blue fabric (or whatever color you choose) for the green fabric mentioned in the following instructions.

To save time cutting "branches," place a 15 × 11-inch piece of white fabric on top of a matching piece of green fabric, right sides facing. Fold the two pieces in half to 7½ × 11 inches (with the white fabric on the outside) and treat all four layers as one piece. In this way it will be possible to cut out four pieces at one time, and the white and green pieces will be facing each other, ready to sew together.

Use Strip A (page 190) to mark four parallel lines across the fabric. Place pattern piece #5 between the parallel lines and mark off triangles with eight across each row, making four rows of eight triangles each. See Diagram 1. Pin the layers together in the center of every other triangle to keep the fabric from shifting. Cut out the triangles. (You may have to cut some extra white triangles for certain designs.)

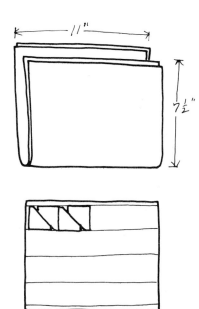

Diagram 1. Cut "branches" or "feathers."

One tree.

Piecing Diagrams

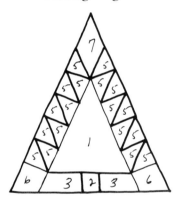

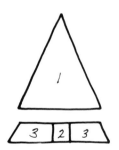

Diagram 2. Assemble basic tree.

Note: Be sure to mark and cut accurately, especially when you are making any of the Feathered Star designs, since blocks made up of many pieces tend to "grow." Check the stacks of triangles after you have cut them to make sure that extra seam allowance wasn't added when you were marking the fabric. Trim to pattern piece if necessary.

SEWING INSTRUCTIONS

Cut and sew one piece #3 to one side of each piece #2. Press the seams open.

Sew a second piece #3 to the other side of each piece #2. Press the seams open.

Sew one piece #1 to the top of each section completed above. Press the seams open. See Diagram 2.

Set aside 16 white #5 pieces to use later. Pin and sew one of the remaining white #5's to each green #5 along the diagonal (bias) side. See Diagram 3. Press the seams open. You should have a total of 64 green and white squares.

Sew four of the green and white squares together in a row. Repeat for a total of eight rows. Press the seams open.

Now, sew four green and white squares together in a row so that the green triangles point in the opposite direction from those completed above. See Diagram 4. Repeat for eight rows. Press the seams open.

Sew one of the 16 white triangles (#5) you had set aside to the top of each completed row of squares so that it points in the same direction as the other white triangles in the row.

Diagram 3. Stitch green and white triangles together on the diagonal to form squares.

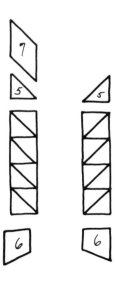

Diagram 4. Stitch pieced squares together into rows.

Sew one white piece #6 to the bottom of each row facing the direction shown, with the long side outside. Press the seams open.

Sew one green diamond (piece #7) to the top of each left-hand row of squares. Press the seams open.

Sew a right-hand row of pieced squares to the right side of each tree, matching the seams at the intersections as indicated by the arrow. Press the seams to one side, toward the tree.

Now, sew a left-hand row of pieced squares with piece #7 at the top, to the left side of each tree, matching the seams at the intersections. Press the seams toward the tree. See Diagram 5.

To assemble the block: Sew two trees together along one side, matching the points of the branches. Repeat for a total of four pairs. Press the seams open.

Sew two pairs together in the same way. Repeat for the other two pairs. Press the seams open.

Next, sew the two halves together, again matching the tips of the branches and the seams at the center intersections. Press the seams open.

Sew one piece #8, a corner triangle, to the bottom of every other tree to make a square. See Diagram 6. Press the seams to one side away from the trees.

To complete the pillow, see page 33.

Diagram 5. Stitch right-hand row of "branches" to trees.

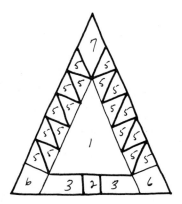

Piecing diagram.

Christmas Pine Quilt

The Christmas Pine Quilt measures 66 × 93½ inches. It requires batting of at least the same size, preferably a little larger. The trees can be made either one at a time in different colors, eight at a time following the instructions for the Christmas Pine Pillow (page 161), or all thirty-two trees can be assembled at once, in stages, following the instructions below.

MATERIALS

Fabric

	ONE TREE
Pattern piece	**Number of pieces**
1	1 green
2	1 green
3	2 white
5	8 green, 10 white
6	2 white
7	1 green

	THIRTY-TWO TREES
Pattern piece	**Number of pieces**
1	32 green
2	32 green
3	64 white
5	256 green, 320 white
6	64 white
7	32 green

Also cut:

31 triangles (pattern piece #9)

14 half-triangles (pattern piece #9A)

2 green borders 5 × 63 inches

2 green borders 5 × 46½ inches

2 cranberry borders 11 × 72 inches

2 cranberry borders 11 × 67 inches

9 yards of 2-inch-wide green bias trim to make a ½-inch border

5¼ yards of cranberry backing fabric

Note: To save time cutting "branches" (piece #5) for thirty-two trees, see Cutting Branches (page 161). Since these instructions are for eight trees, repeat the process four times to make thirty-two trees.

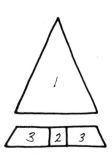

Diagram 1. Assemble basic tree.

Diagram 2. Stitch green and white triangles into squares.

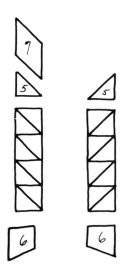

Diagram 3. Stitch pieced squares together into rows.

Diagram 4. Stitch right-hand row of "branches" to tree.

SEWING INSTRUCTIONS

Sew one piece #3 to one side of each piece #2. Press the seams open. Sew a second piece #3 to the other side of each piece #2. Press the seams open.

Sew a piece #1 to the top of each section completed above. See Diagram 1. Press the seams open.

Set aside 64 white triangles (#5) to use later. Pin and sew one of the remaining white #5's to each green piece #5 along the diagonal (bias) side. Press the seams open. You should have a total of 256 green and white pieced squares. See Diagram 2.

Sew four of the green and white squares completed above together in a row. Press the seams open. Repeat for 32 rows.

Sew four green and white squares together in a row so that the green triangles point in the opposite direction from those in the rows constructed above. Press the seams open. Repeat for 32 rows.

Sew one of the remaining white triangles (piece #5) to the top of each completed row of squares so that it points in the same direction as the other white triangles. See Diagram 3.

Sew one white piece #6 to the bottom of each row facing in the direction shown, with the long side outside. Press the seams open.

Sew one green diamond (piece #7) to the top of each left-hand row of squares. Press the seams open.

Sew a right-hand row of pieced squares (#5's) to the right side of the tree, matching the seams at the intersections as indicated by the arrow. Press the seams in one direction toward the tree (center). See Diagram 4.

Sew one of the left-hand rows (with #7) to the left side of each tree, matching the seams at the intersections. Press the seam toward the tree (center).

To assemble the quilt top: Sew the pieced trees and the cranberry triangles (piece #9) and half-triangles (piece #9A) into rows as follows, to create four rows of five trees and three rows of four trees. Press all of the seams toward the triangles. See Diagrams 5 and 6.

Pin and sew all seven rows together, alternating rows of five trees with rows of four trees (there should be a row of five trees at the top and at the bottom). Press the seams away from the trees.

Next, sew a green border, 5 × 63 inches, to each side of the quilt top. Press the seam toward the borders. Sew a green border, 5 × 46½ inches, to the top and bottom of the quilt top. Press the seams toward the borders. See Diagram 7.

In the same way, sew a cranberry border, 11 × 72 inches, to each side of the quilt top. Press the seams toward the cranberry borders. Sew a cranberry border, 11 × 67 inches, to the top and bottom of the quilt top. Press the seams toward the cranberry borders. See Diagram 8.

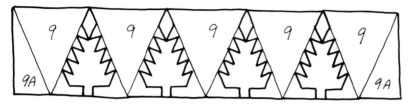

Diagram 5. Row of five trees.

Diagram 6. Row of four trees.

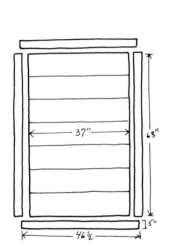

Diagram 7. Add green borders
to quilt top.

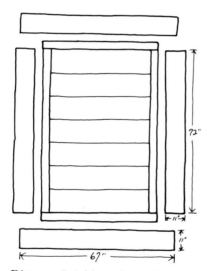

Diagram 8. Add cranberry borders
to quilt top.

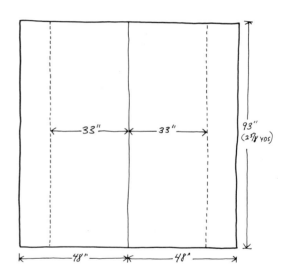

Diagram 9. Assemble back of quilt.

For backing, sew two 2⅝-yard lengths of cranberry fabric together, along the long sides. See Diagram 9. Trim the backing to match the quilt top (approximately 66 × 93 inches). To assemble, layer the quilt top, batting, and back together and pin (pages 18–26).

Suggested quilting patterns: A Double Feather Cable pattern for the inside green borders; a Clamshell pattern for the background; a Double Feather Wreath for the four corners. This Christmas Pine was quilted with cranberry thread.

Star and Pine Quilt

This small quilt or wall hanging is made with an eight-pointed star in the center, surrounded by eight of the Christmas Pine trees (page 161). This time, the trees are arranged to point outward, rather than in toward the center of the design. However, they are made in exactly the same way, with the exception that pattern piece #3A is substituted for pattern piece #3.

MATERIALS

Fabric

STAR AND PINES

Pattern piece	Number of pieces
1	8 green
2	8 green
3A	16 white
5	64 green, 64 white
7	8 green
10	8 white
11 (or 11A)	8 red (16 red)

FOLDED RIBBON BORDER

Pattern piece	Number of pieces
1	36 green
2	72 white
3	32 red

Other Materials

2 white borders, 8½ × 27½ inches

2 white borders, 8½ × 44 inches

45-inch square of batting (or a slightly larger square)

45-inch square of white backing fabric

5 yards of red 2-inch bias trim to make ½-inch binding for the outer edge

Note: To save time cutting out "branches" see Cutting Branches (page 161).

SEWING INSTRUCTIONS

Sew one piece #3A to one side of each piece #2. Press the seams open. Sew a second piece #3A to the other side of each piece #2. Press the seams open.

Sew a piece #1 to the top of each section completed above. See Diagram 1. Press the seams open.

Set aside sixteen white and sixteen green triangles (piece #5) to use later. Sew a white piece #5 to each of the remaining green #5's along the diagonal

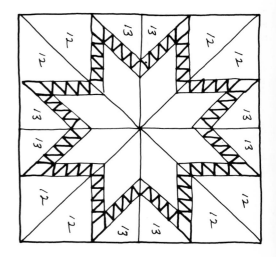

Piecing diagrams.

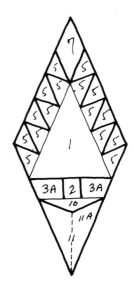

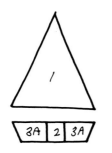

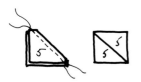

Diagram 1. Assemble basic tree.

(bias) side. See Diagram 2. Press the seams open. You should now have a total of 48 pieced green and white squares.

Sew three sets of pieced green and white squares together in a row. See Diagram 3. Press the seams open. Repeat for a total of eight rows. Now, sew three sets of squares together in a row with points facing in the opposite direction. Repeat for a total of eight rows. Press the seams open.

Sew a green piece #5 (set aside earlier) to the bottom of each row so that it points in the same direction as the other green triangles in the row. Sew a white piece #5 to the top of each row so that it points in the same direction as the other white triangles in the row. Press the seams open. Sew a piece #7 (green diamond) to the top of each left-hand row. Press the seams open.

Sew a right-hand row of #5's to the right side of each tree. Press the seams in one direction, away from the tree. Sew a left-hand row of #5's to the left side of each tree, matching the seams at the top point of each piece #1. See Diagram 4. Press the seams away from the tree.

To make the bottom of the diamond (⅛ of the block): Sew one piece #10 to each piece #11 with piece #10 on top. To turn the corner at the center of piece #11 (or between two #11A pieces), leave the needle down and lift the presser foot. Clip the seam allowance on piece #11 up to the needle. Pivot and adjust the fabric. Lower the presser foot and continue sewing.

Diagram 2. Stitch triangles into squares.

Note: To add interest, pattern piece #11A can be substituted for pattern piece #11 for use with stripes or two colors, as in quilt on page 168. Take care to match the seams at the intersections, particularly at the center.

Sew the 10-11 sections to the bottom of each pieced tree. Press the seams open. See Diagram 5.

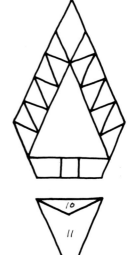

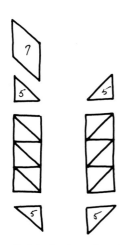

Diagram 3. Stitch pieced squares and triangle together into rows.

Diagram 4. Stitch "branches" to trees.

Diagram 5. Complete diamond segment of quilt block.

Sew one piece #12 (large triangle) to the right-hand side of four of the trees completed above. Sew a piece #12 to the left-hand side of the other four trees. Press the seams toward the triangles (#12's).

Sew a piece #13 (smaller triangle) to the remaining sides of all eight trees. Press the seams toward the #13's. See Diagram 6.

Sew two trees together along the sides to which the #12's are sewn, matching the seams at the intersections, to create a square. Repeat for a total of four squares. Press the seams open. See Diagram 7.

Sew two of these squares together creating two halves, matching the seams at the intersections. Press the seams open.

Sew the two halves of the star together, carefully matching the seams at the center and the other intersections. See piecing diagram, page 169.

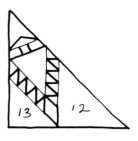

Diagram 6. Sew one #12 to right-hand side of four trees. Sew one #12 to left-hand side of other four trees. Sew one #13 to remaining side of all trees.

Folded Ribbon Border

Set aside four piece #1's and eight piece #2's to use later. Sew a square (piece #1) to one side of each of thirty-two triangles (piece #2) so that sixteen triangles face one direction and sixteen face the other direction. Press the seams open. See Diagram 8.

Sew a second white triangle (#2) to the opposite side of each green square (piece #1). See Diagram 9. Press the seams open.

Sew a red piece #3 to one side of each section completed above. See Diagram 10. Press the seams open.

Sew four of each pieced set together in a row. Four rows will slant in one direction and four in the other. Press the seams open.

Sew a piece #2 to one side of each of the remaining four squares (piece #1). Press the seams open. Sew a piece #2 to the adjoining side of the piece #1. See Diagram 11. Press the seams open.

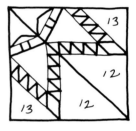

Diagram 7. Sew two trees together along sides with #12 pieces to make square.

Make 16   Make 16

Diagram 8. Stitch triangles (#2) to 32 squares (#1).

Diagram 9. Add a second #2 to opposite sides of each #1.

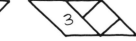

Diagram 10. Stitch a #3 to one side, 16 to the right, 16 to the left.

Diagram 11. Stitch a #2 to each side of one corner on a #1.

171

Sew each one of these sections between two pieced rows going in opposite directions to create four Folded Ribbon Border pieces. See Diagram 12. Press the seams open.

Sew a Folded Ribbon Border piece to opposite sides of the quilt top, stopping ¼ inch from the end of the border at the corners. Press the seams away from the border.

Sew the other two Folded Ribbon Border pieces to the other sides of the quilt top, turning the corners at the ends and matching the seams at the intersections. Press the seams away from the border.

To finish quilt: Sew two white borders, 8½ × 27½ inches, to opposite sides of the quilt top. Press the seams away from the Folded Ribbon Border.

Sew the two white borders, 8½ × 44 inches, to top and bottom of quilt top. Press seams away from Folded Ribbon Border. See Diagram 13.

To assemble:

Layer and pin the quilt top, batting and backing together. For further instructions, see pages 18–26.

Suggested quilt patterns: Feather Wreath for the corner squares; Half Feather Wreath for the triangles at the center sides; and a Feather Scroll for the borders.

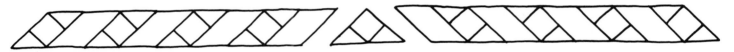

Diagram 12. Piece together Folded Ribbon Border.   Make 4

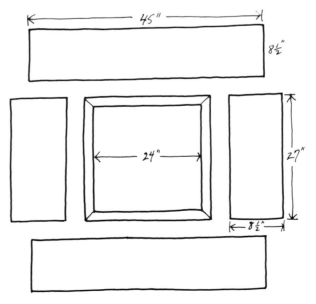

Diagram 13. Add borders.

Simple Feathered Star

It is a good idea for beginners to make this simple star first, before tackling the more complex stars in the Feathered Star Quilt.

MATERIALS

Fabric

Pattern piece	ONE STAR Number of pieces
5	64 blue, 64 white
7	8 blue
12	8 white
13	8 white
14	8 blue

Note: To save time cutting out "feathers" see Cutting Branches (page 161).

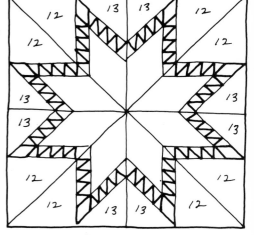

Piecing diagrams.

SEWING INSTRUCTIONS

Set aside sixteen pairs of white and blue triangles (piece #5) to use later. Sew a white piece #5 to each of the remaining blue #5's along the diagonal side. You should have a total of 48 pieced blue and white squares. Press the seams open. See Diagram 1.

Sew three sets of pieced squares together in a row. See Diagram 2. Repeat for a total of eight rows. Press the seams open.

Sew three sets of squares together in a row with the points of the blue triangles facing in the opposite direction. Repeat for a total of eight rows. Press the seams open.

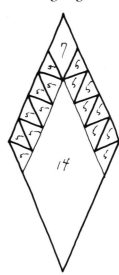

Diagram 1. Stitch triangle together to form squares.

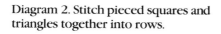

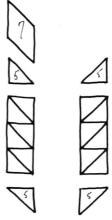

Diagram 2. Stitch pieced squares and triangles together into rows.

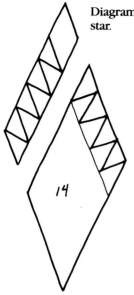

Diagram 3. Stitch "feathers" to point of star.

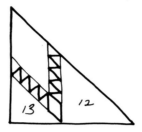

Diagram 4. Sew one #12 to right side of four points. Sew one #12 to left side of other four points. Sew one #13 to remaining side of all points.

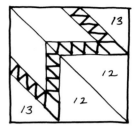

Diagram 5. Sew two points together along sides with #12 pieces to make square.

Sew a white piece #5 to the top of each right-hand row so that it points in the same direction as the other white triangles in the row. Sew a blue piece #5 to the bottom of each row so that it points in the same direction as the other blue triangles in the row. Press the seams open.

Sew a blue diamond (piece #7) to the top of each left-hand row of squares. Press the seams open.

Sew a right-hand row of squares to the upper right side of each piece #14. Press the seams toward the #14's. Sew a left-hand row of squares to the upper left side of each piece #14, matching the seams at the top point of each #14. See Diagram 3. Press the seams toward the #14's.

Sew a piece #12 to the right side of four of the points of the star completed above. Sew a piece #12 to the left side of the four other points. Press the seams in one direction, toward the #12's.

Sew a piece #13 to the other sides of the points, opposite the #12's. Press the seams toward the #13's. See Diagram 4.

Sew two points together along the sides to which the #12's are sewn, matching the seams at the intersections to create one square. Repeat for a total of four squares. Press the seams open. See Diagram 5.

Sew two of these squares together to create two halves of the star, matching the seams at the intersections. Press the seams open.

Sew the two halves of the star together, matching the seams at the center and the other intersections. See piecing diagram. Press the seams open.

To finish the Simple Feathered Star as a pillow, see Assembling the Pillow Top, page 33.

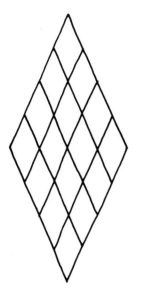

Diagram 1. Each point is made up of 16 parts.

Feathered Star

The Feathered Star designs are really just an extension of the Simple Feathered Star. The diamond in the center of each point is subdivided to create more complex designs — the greater number of pieces, the more complex the design. A very beautiful quilt could be made with twelve blocks of the same star design, with a combination of several different stars, or with each star unique. I used blue and white fabrics with a touch of red for this Feathered Star. You can use any colors you like.

Each diamond segment (⅛ of one star) has been divided into sixteen pieces. See Diagram 1.

As many as all sixteen of these pieces can be used, or any combination of them. Diagram 2 suggests a few of the design possibilities and describes the order in which the pieces are assembled.

Use the drawings on page 178 as work sheets to plan your own color schemes for the Feathered Star. Color them with felt-tip, water-base markers in whatever way you find appealing. Feel free to experiment with your own designs. Remember that there are pattern pieces that correspond in size to areas that contain one to four diamonds in a row (pattern pieces #17 through #20) or areas that consist of four, nine, and sixteen diamonds (pattern pieces #14, #15, and #16). For example, the design in Diagram 3 requires three patterns: #15, #17, and #19.

To determine how many pieces are needed for one star, multiply the number of pieces in one diamond by eight.

Pattern piece	Number of pieces
15	8
17	8
19	16

To save time cutting out pieces #17, #18, #19, and #20, use Strip B to mark parallel lines. Then place diamond-shaped patterns between the lines, mark and cut.

Following are instructions for a Feathered Star Quilt with twelve stars, a Folded Ribbon Border and a 12-inch-wide outer border. The quilt measures 99 × 123½ inches.

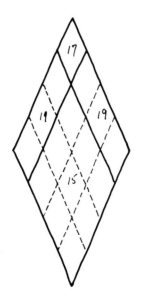

Diagram 3. This design requires pattern pieces #15, #17 and #19.

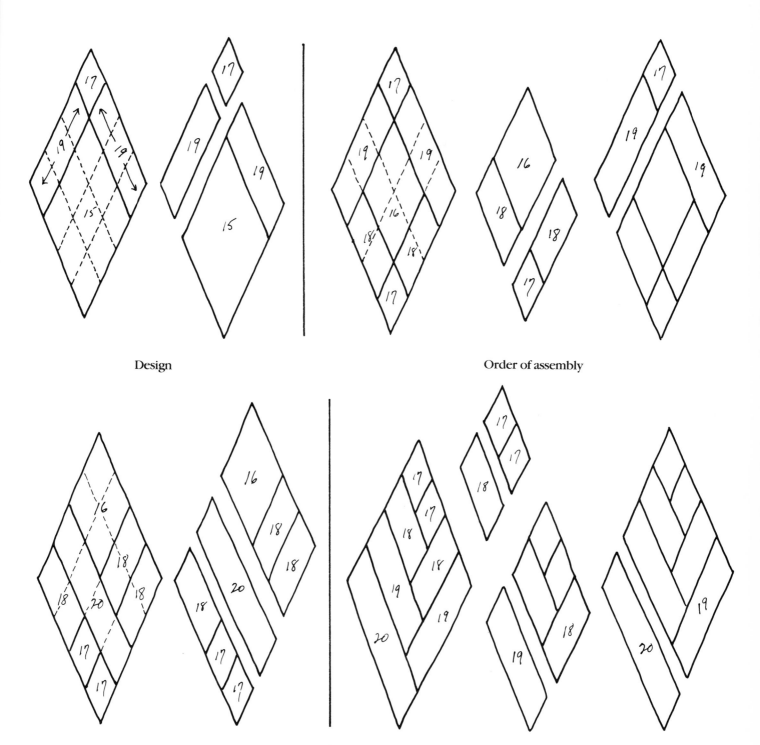

Design   Order of assembly

Diagram 2. Various ways to assemble pattern pieces to make points.

177

Use drawings below to plan color scheme. Color with water-base colored markers, medium point.

MATERIALS

Fabric

FEATHERED STAR

(Blue and white print fabrics, vary them according to your own preference for each star)

9 yards of 48-inch-wide backing fabric

Pattern piece	Number of pieces
12	96
13	96

Four 12½ × 99½-inch strips for the outer border

FOLDED RIBBON BORDER

Pattern piece	Number of pieces
1	116 dark blue
2	232 white
3	112 blue

Other Materials

12¼ yards of 2-inch bias trim to make a ½-inch-wide border

Batting

SEWING INSTRUCTIONS

Assemble the diamond sections of each star according to the desired designs. Accurate cutting and sewing are essential. It is also important to match the seams carefully at all of the intersections during assembly to achieve the best results.

Cut and add "feathers" as described for the Simple Feathered Star (page 161). Add the corner pieces (#12 and #13) to complete the squares. Once all of the squares are finished they can be assembled as a quilt top of three squares across and four down, or whatever configuration is desired.

Folded Ribbon Border

The instructions that follow are for a Folded Ribbon Border for a quilt with twelve stars.

Set aside four piece #1's and eight piece #2's to use later.

Sew a piece #2 to one side of each piece #1 so that 56 triangles face one direction and 56 point in the other direction. Press the seams open. See Diagram 4.

Sew a piece #2 to the other side of each piece #1. Press the seams open. See Diagram 5.

Make 56   Make 56

Diagram 4. Stitch triangles (#2) to squares (#1).

Diagram 5. Add a second #2 to opposite sides of each #1.

Sew a piece #3 to one side of each of the sections completed above. Press the seams open. See Diagram 6.

Sew these sections together into strips as follows: two sets of twelve facing right, two sets of twelve facing left, two sets of sixteen facing right, two sets of sixteen facing left. Press the seams open. See Diagram 7.

Sew a piece #2 to one side of the four #1's set aside earlier. Press the seams open.

Sew a piece #2 to the other side of the adjacent corner of each piece #1. See Diagram 8. Press the seams open.

Sew one of these sections between two strips of twelve 2-1-2 going in opposite directions. Repeat.

Sew another 2-1-2 section between two strips of sixteen in the same way. Press the seams open. This completes four Folded Ribbon Border pieces: two of twenty-four sections, two of thirty-two sections.

Sew the shorter borders to the top and bottom of the quilt top. So that the ends can be mitered, stop stitching ¼ inch from the ends. Press the seams away from the border.

Sew the longer borders to each side of the quilt top in the same way. Press the seams away from the border.

Hand-stitch the ends together at each of the four corners. Press the seams open.

Sew a 12½ × 99½-inch border to each side of the quilt top. Press the seams away from the Folded Ribbon Border.

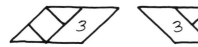

Diagram 6. Stitch a #3 to each section, 56 to the right, 56 to the left.

Diagram 7. Stitch sections together in rows: 2 rows each of 12 to the right and 12 to the left; 2 rows each of 16 to the right and 16 to the left.

Diagram 8. Stitch a #2 to each side of one corner on a #1.

Sew a 12½ × 99 ½-inch border to the top and bottom of the quilt top. Press the seams away from the Folded Ribbon Border. See Diagram 9.

For the back, sew three 3½-yard lengths of 48-inch-wide white fabric together along the sides. Press the seams open. See Diagram 10.

To assemble:

Layer and pin the quilt top, batting and backing together. For instructions in assembling the quilt see pages 18–26.

Suggested quilt patterns: A Feather Wreath for the larger and smaller squares (Half Wreaths for the triangles at the borders), and a Feather Scroll for the borders.

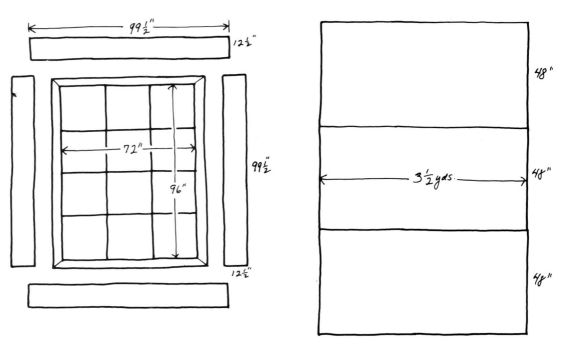

Diagram 9. Add borders.   Diagram 10. Piece backing.

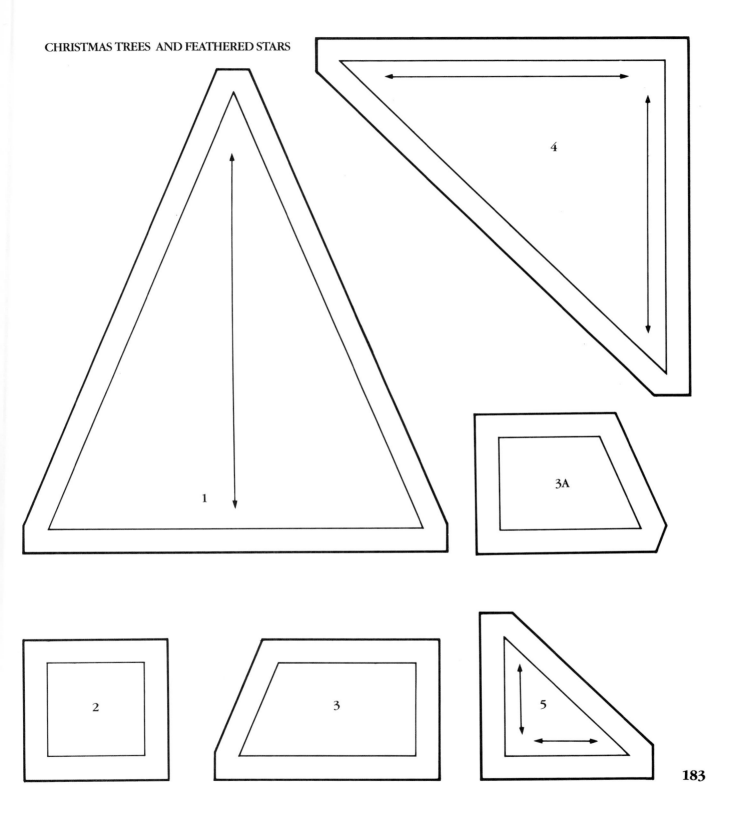

1

4

3A

2

3

5

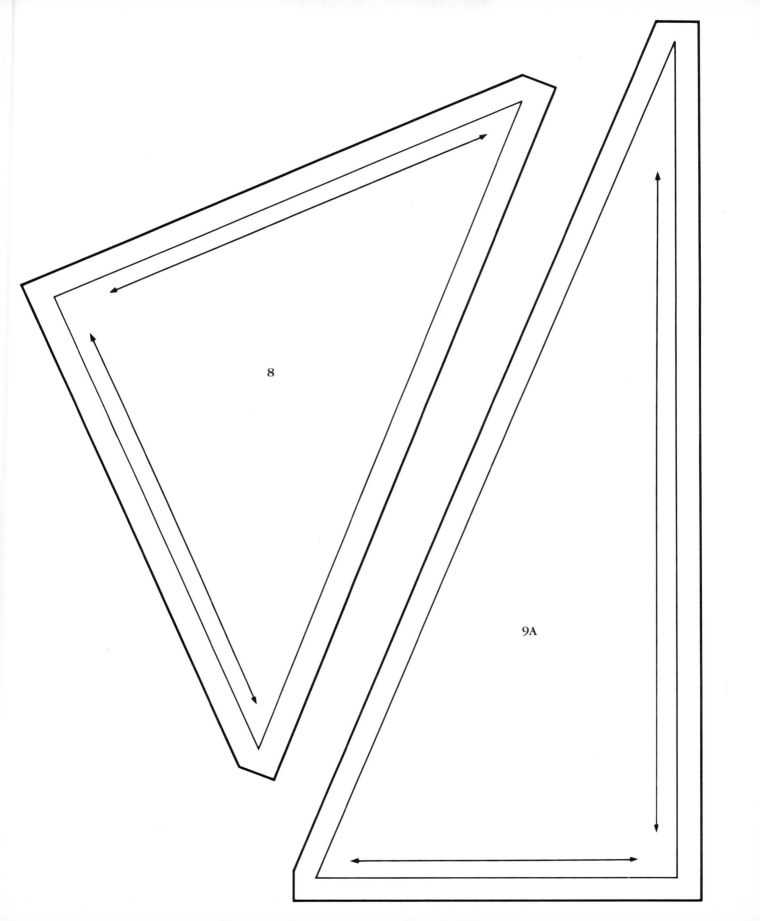

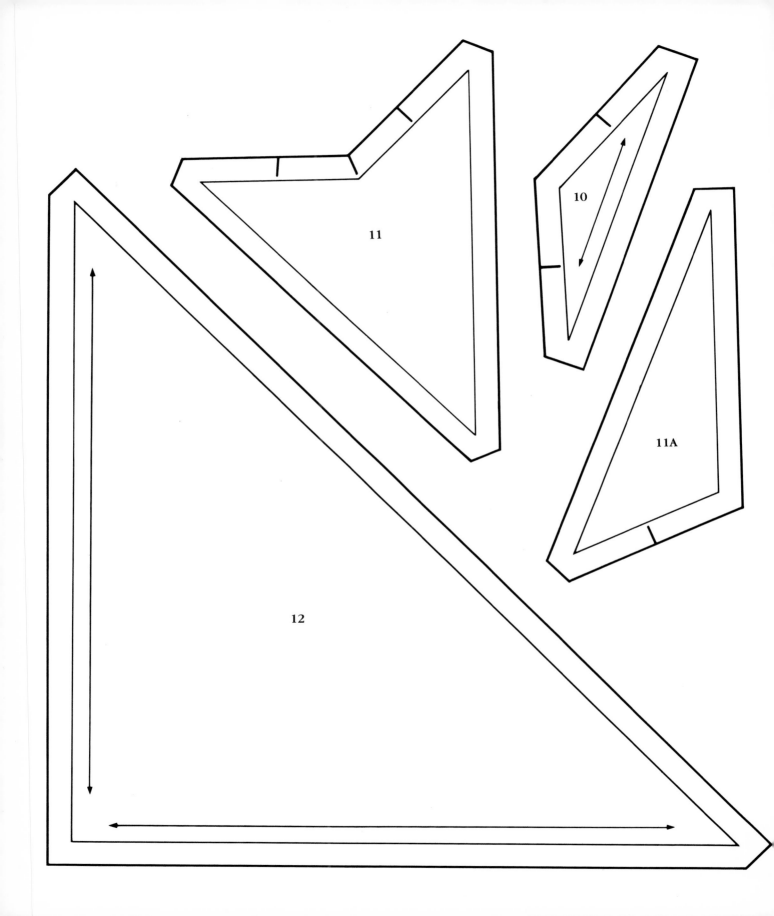

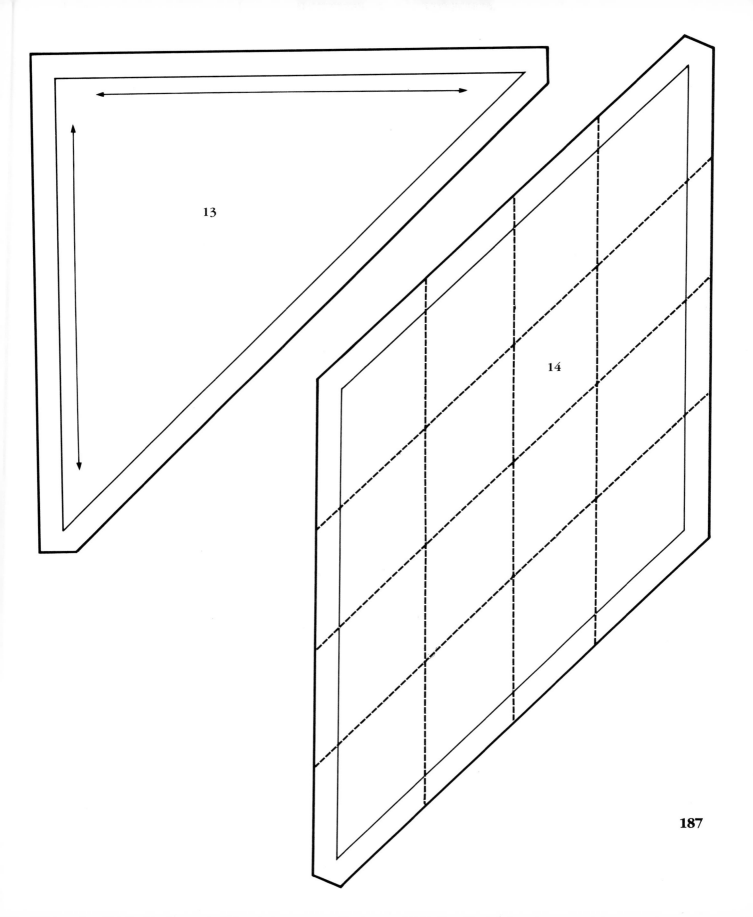

13

14

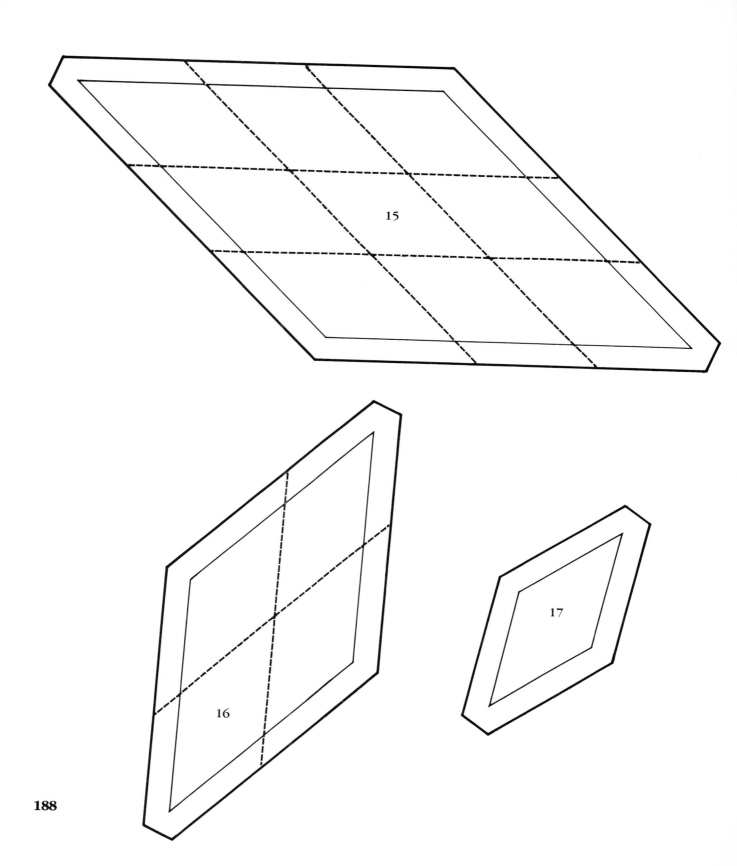

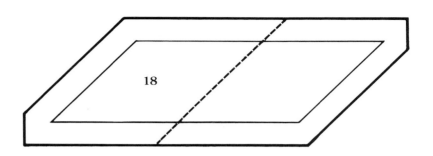

18

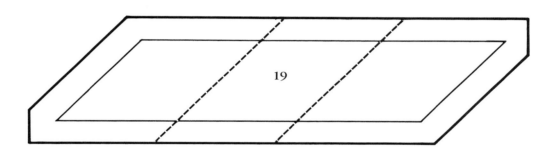

19

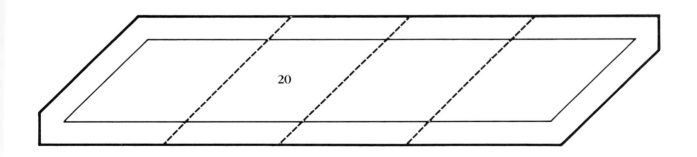

20

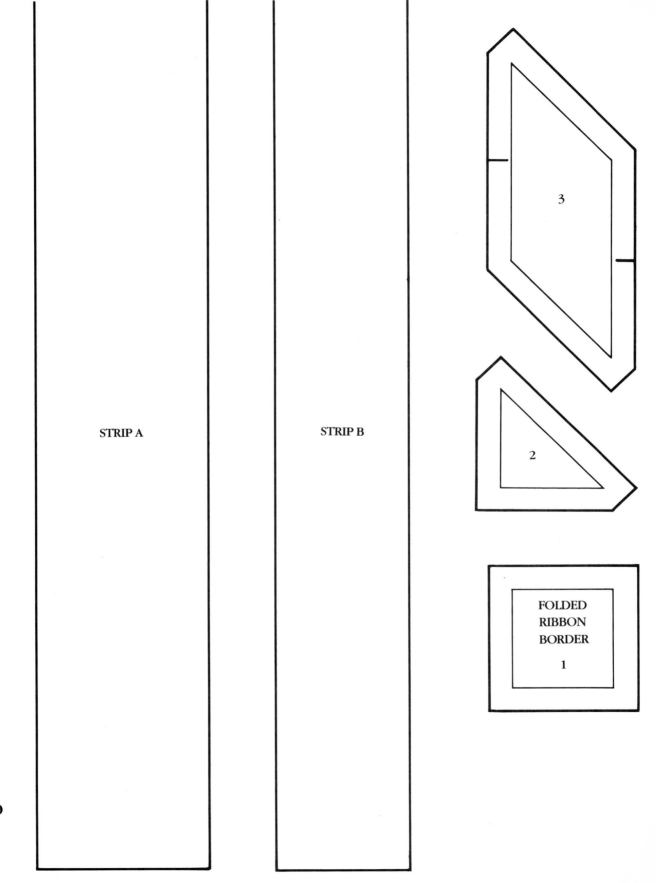

STRIP A

STRIP B

3

2

FOLDED
RIBBON
BORDER

1

190

INDEX

(Page references in **bold face** type indicate illustrations)